CONNECTICUT BASEBALL

THE BEST
OF THE
NUTMEG STATE

DON HARRISON

FOREWORD BY FAY VINCENT

Charleston — London

THE
History
PRESS

Published by The History Press
Charleston, SC 29403
www.historypress.net

Cover design by Natasha Momberger

First published 2008

Manufactured in the United States

ISBN 978.1.59629.552.0

Library of Congress Cataloging-in-Publication Data

Harrison, Don.
Connecticut baseball : the best of the nutmeg state / Don Harrison.
p. cm.
Includes bibliographical references.
ISBN 978-1-59629-552-0
1. Baseball--Connecticut--History. I. Title.
GV863.C8H37 2008
796.35709746--dc22

2008032137

CONTENTS

FOREWORD

I was born in Waterbury, and I share some passions with Don Harrison. We both love our lovely Connecticut and we are devoted to our game. I say "our game" because he and I, and millions of others, believe we own this magical game. We know there are a few financial giants who think they own the teams, and they are legally correct. But we know we own the game because for us baseball exists as much in our minds, and especially in our memories, as it does on the balance sheets of those often tasteless moguls.

Harrison served for a time as the sports editor of the *Waterbury Republican*. He was successor to such greats as Bill Slocum, Dan Parker and Hank O'Donnell. It was his good fortune to cover nine World Series, to be present for the Mets' victory over the favored Orioles in 1969 and to witness Reggie Jackson's three home runs in the final game of the 1977 World Series. This book is the product of a lifetime of writing about the many superb baseball players from our state.

Baseball is essentially a local game. We love our local teams, and my friend Bart Giamatti often noted that there is an imaginary line through the center of our state that runs through New Haven and divides the Yankees West from the Red Sox East.

There, right on that line, I grew up with memories of the likes of Jimmy Piersall, also from Waterbury, and Walt Dropo from Moosup, both of whom played for the Red Sox, while Spec Shea of Naugatuck pitched for the Yankees. Younger readers will recall Steve Blass, Mo Vaughn, Charles Nagy and Bobby Valentine.

There is a long and illustrious line of great players from the tiny Nutmeg State, and Harrison has lovingly assembled this compendium of interviews with twenty-five of the most prominent. He also picks the best players from Connecticut (you are free to disagree with him) and is careful not to ignore the fine set of Connecticut umpires, including Ed Rapuano, Terry Tata, the Hirschbeck brothers and Frank Dascoli.

It is books like this one that separate baseball from other sports, for we who own this game cannot stop thinking about it and how much we care about it. We are undeterred by those who decry it or try to harm it. We know it cannot be touched because it remains secure in what Bart called "the green fields of our minds."

This fine little book takes you right to that green field. Enjoy the trip.

Fay Vincent
Commissioner of Baseball, 1989–1992

ACKNOWLEDGEMENTS

First and foremost, my deepest appreciation goes to Saunders Robinson, who wears the dual mantle of northeast publisher and senior commissioning editor at The History Press, for believing in this project and for providing expert guidance and encouragement along the way. Initially, she felt it was a "little out of our comfort zone," but once she came onboard—wow! Thank you.

Jaime Muehl, project editor at The History Press, made valuable modifications to the manuscript, and for that I am thankful. Born and raised in Cooperstown, New York, Jaime has baseball in her roots, which seems providential, don't you think?

I am indebted to several people for supplying the majority of the older images: from the Library of Congress, Erica Kelly; from the National Baseball Hall of Fame Library, John W. Horne Jr.; from the Connecticut Historical Society, Nancy Finlay, curator of graphics; from the Connecticut State Library, Mel Smith, archivist; and from the Mattatuck Historical Society, Suzie Fateh, collections manager, and Cynthia Roznoy, curator. Elizabeth von Tuyl of the Bridgeport Public Library's Historical Collections provided valuable research assistance.

Our managing editor at the *Greenwich Citizen*, Gary Jeanfaivre, was kind enough to share several of his baseball cards and to provide valuable input on the new material.

ACKNOWLEDGEMENTS

Patty Hayman, niece of the late John "Pretzels" Pezzullo, was gracious enough to track down and share the photo of her uncle.

Tom Kabelka, for several years the photo editor at the *Waterbury Republican-American* during my tenure and a good friend as well, allowed me to use his photos of Dave Parker and Fred Lynn.

I also extend my thanks to our most recent intern from Greenwich High School, Laura Carlson, for her typing and unfailing good nature.

INTRODUCTION

If not for the kindness and patience of three men, this book—and perhaps all of the columns, game reports and features that preceded this book—might not have seen the light of day.

I was two weeks shy of my twenty-first birthday when I entered a world of journalistic giants at the *New York Mirror*. My resume revealed that I was a college dropout and the author of two unfinished, unpublished works: a novel about a teenage gang and a largely statistical book about the Brooklyn Dodgers. The people in the *Mirror* personnel office, placing greater stock in my compilation of Dodger numbers, assigned me to the sports department.

The sports staff that I joined in late summer was two dozen strong, ranging from a superstar sports columnist and sports editor, Dan Parker, to three copy boys, and I became the junior member. Parker, although approaching his seventieth year, was as prolific as he was gifted; he produced seven columns each and every week.

The *Mirror* was a mixture of lurid headlines and horse-racing results; a saucy tabloid long before the advent of supermarket tabloids. Its daily circulation hovered around 900,000. On Sunday, more than 1.2 million copies were sold. "The second largest circulation of any daily newspaper in the country," proclaimed the *Mirror*'s house ads.

Walter Winchell was the unchallenged star. Although on the downside of a career that had catapulted him to unsurpassed heights as a gossip columnist and radio personality, Winchell remained the undisputed king of the three-dot profession, the most powerful and controversial newsman in print and on the air.

I was assigned the night shift, 6:00 p.m. to 1:00 a.m., and was informed that Tuesday and Wednesday would be my days off. My major duties consisted of monitoring the AP and UPI sports wires, "stripping" each wire and placing the news items in the "in" basket on the night sports editor's desk.

The man who filled this role on most occasions was a gem, Frank Kearns. Kind and helpful, he would spend hours after deadline drumming into my head the elements of style, editing my feeble writing attempts and reminiscing about his years at the old *Brooklyn Eagle*.

Parker worked the day shift when he wasn't out on assignment, and so a week or two was to elapse before I glimpsed the great columnist for the first time. "Don't worry," George Girsch, a sports copy editor, had assured me. "You'll know him when you see him."

Sure enough, Parker entered the City Room late one afternoon or early one evening (I don't recall which), and there he was, six feet, four and weighing, well, a lot. His facial features were familiar from his column photo, but I was stunned to see that he was so huge.

When we finally had the opportunity to chat, he was pleased to learn that I, too, had grown up in Connecticut. Born and reared in Waterbury, Dan had worked as sports editor of the *Waterbury Republican* prior to his arrival in New York during the mid-1920s.

We struck up a man-boy friendship. After reading some of the early chapters of my proposed book, *Home Runs Unlimited*, he agreed to write the foreword and offered some leads with publishers. I was overwhelmed by his kindness.

At some point during the evening, I was expected to make a food run for the department, generally to the A&M restaurant on the opposite side of East Forty-fifth Street. Even at this late date, I recall one such mission with a tinge of embarrassment.

Arthur Richman, a baseball writer, had requested an egg cream on this particular night. A what? Being raised in the distant precincts of Connecticut, I was totally unfamiliar with this New York City soda fountain favorite. I returned and handed Arthur a bag containing what I thought he had requested…an egg salad sandwich. He was mildly annoyed, but, much to my relief, greatly amused.

Arthur was to provide me with considerable guidance and encouragement, and we've remained in touch, first when he handled public relations for the New York Mets and later when he became a special adviser to George Steinbrenner with the New York Yankees.

My stay at the *Mirror* was to last three years, a period divided between my copy boy stint and elevation to sports deskman. I wrote a few bylined features, but mainly I was entrusted with editing copy and supervising the "make-up" of the sports pages in the Composing Room.

The end came with surprising suddenness. On October 15, 1963, citing "costs (that) have risen far in excess of revenues and have created substantial deficits over an extended period of time," the Hearst Corporation announced the closing of its morning tabloid. The paper's name and many of its assets were sold to the rival *New York Daily News*.

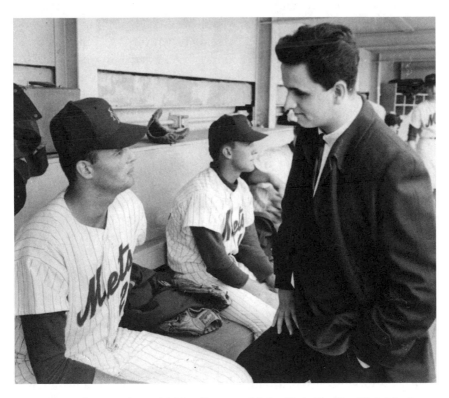

Author Don Harrison chats with Tom Parsons of Lakeville in the New York Mets' dugout at Shea Stadium, April 1965. *Courtesy of the* Waterbury Republican/*Greg Chilson*.

INTRODUCTION

Happily, my apprenticeship had prepared me well for future endeavors. Parker informed me of an opening at his old paper in Waterbury, and that's where my career resumed (with just four working days lost in the transition). With the exception of a two-year hiatus at the *New Haven Journal-Courier*, I would spend the next eighteen years with the *Republican*, being appointed sports editor in 1968 and then, in 1977, executive sports editor of the *Waterbury Republican-American*.

Baseball was my sport of choice. During this period, I was given the opportunity to cover nine World Series, several American League playoffs, one National League playoff and, joy of joys, to make annual treks to Florida to cover the spring training camps. There were interviews with many of the game's greatest, from Reggie Jackson (on the night he hit three home runs against the Dodgers in the final game of the 1977 World Series) to George Brett, from Smoky Joe Wood and Bob Feller to Dixie Walker and Jim Palmer.

I was just twenty-five years old when I was assigned to my first World Series—game three of the 1964 Series between the St. Louis Cardinals and the mighty Yankees at Yankee Stadium. It ended in dramatic fashion, on Mickey Mantle's Series-record sixteenth home run in the bottom of the ninth inning. Score: Yankees three, Cardinals two. Five years later, I was at Shea Stadium to chronicle the Mets' improbable Series triumph over the heavily favored Baltimore Orioles.

A chance encounter with James T. Farrell, author of the Studs Lonigan trilogy, one spring in Fort Lauderdale led to an interview in his room at the Gault Ocean Mile and a Sunday column.

One of my favorite pieces was a January 1981 interview with Joe Pepitone, conducted in the backseat of an automobile for as long as it took to travel from Yankee Stadium to Waterbury, Connecticut. Talk about a captive subject.

Much later, after I'd made the transition to public relations at Sacred Heart University in Fairfield, Connecticut, at my request Richman became one of the notable participants—along with Cardinal John O'Connor, Curt Gowdy, Marty Glickman and Suzyn Waldman—in an interfaith memorial service for Mel Allen at St. Patrick's Cathedral. Yogi Berra and Phil Rizzuto were among the one thousand in attendance. The November 4, 1996 tribute to the Hall of Fame broadcaster was orchestrated by Rabbi Joseph Ehrenkranz of the university's Center for Christian-Jewish Understanding (CCJU). Ehrenkranz was Mel's friend and rabbi.

INTRODUCTION

I trust you will enjoy this collection of interviews that took place over a forty-three-year period. The lion's share appeared in the *Waterbury Republican*, but several were written for the *New York Times*'s Connecticut section and a lively but short-lived weekly, the *Bridgeport Light*. Still others were gathered for the *New Haven Journal-Courier*, the *Fairfield Citizen-News* and, most recently, the weekly *Greenwich Citizen*, which, as founding editor, I had the privilege to help launch in 2002.

So, a heartfelt thank you to Messrs. Dan Parker, Arthur Richman and Frank Kearns. You helped to make it all possible.

CHAPTER 1

PLAYING THE GAME

L ong before the Hartford Whalers brought the National Hockey League to Connecticut, the state's capital city was major league in another sport: baseball. For most of us, this will come as a surprise since it happened more than 130 years ago.

In the summer of 1876, the Hartford Dark Blues became one of the founding members of the National League, the same league we know today in Major League Baseball. Not only that, but Morgan G. Bulkeley, who was president of the Dark Blues during their two seasons (1874–75) in the not-quite-major-league National Association, was elected unanimously as the league's first president. He was credited with enhancing the game's image by curtailing gambling and drinking.

Later, Bulkeley would become much wider known as a two-term mayor of Hartford, governor of Connecticut and then a United States senator. In 1937, he was among the second group of players and executives elected to the National Baseball Hall of Fame in Cooperstown, New York.

The Dark Blues performed well in 1876, finishing third in the eight-team National League with a record of 47–21. Ahead of them were the pennant-winning Chicago White Stockings (forerunners of the Chicago Cubs) and the second-place St. Louis Brown Stockings. The team's home games were played at the Hartford Base Ball Grounds, located near the Church of the Good Shepherd on Wyllys Street.

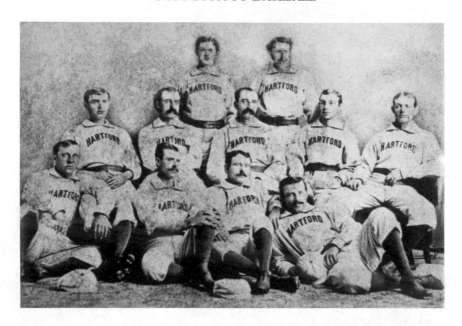

The Hartford Dark Blues were a charter member of the National League in 1876. *Back row, standing*: Tommy Bond, Candy Cummings. *Middle row*: Tom Carey, Everett Mills, Bob Ferguson (player-manager), Bill Harbidge, Tommy York. *Front row, seated*: Dick Higham, Jack Burdock, Jack Remsen, Doug Allison. *T.J. Kirkpatrick photo/Courtesy of the Connecticut State Library, Hartford, Connecticut.*

The Dark Blues' forte was pitching—and just two men shared the workload. Tommy Bond, a native of Granard, Ireland, compiled a 31–13 record and completed all forty-five of his starts. Arthur "Candy" Cummings, best known as the originator of the curveball, did the rest, finishing with a 16–8 mark and twenty-four complete games. In 1939, Cummings was inducted into the Hall of Fame for his innovation.

At bat, Dick Higham was the club's leader, accumulating a .327 average as the right fielder and part-time catcher. Higham's name endures in infamy; in 1882, he became the first, and only, major league umpire to be expelled for dishonesty.

Unfortunately, the Dark Blues' stay in Hartford was short-lived. Struggling financially, the team was lured to Brooklyn, a major market, for the 1877 season. Bulkeley's successor as league president, William Hulbert, sweetened the deal by allowing the transplanted Hartford club to keep a larger share of the gate receipts than was standard at the time. Brooklyn, with a population of some 600,000, offered a much larger payout than Hartford, which had some 40,000 residents.

As author David Arcidiacono pointed out in his 2003 book, *Grace, Grit and Growling: The Hartford Dark Blues Base Ball Club, 1874–1877*, "This historic agreement made the Dark Blues the first club to change cities without a change in ownership, predating by over 80 years the infamous move of the Dodgers from Brooklyn to Los Angeles."

If Connecticut was left without Major League Baseball, professional baseball would flourish on the minor league level throughout the Nutmeg State in the summers to come. Hartford, New Haven, Waterbury and Bridgeport became hotbeds, each fielding successful teams in the remainder of the nineteenth century and for much of the twentieth century. Stamford and smaller communities such as New Britain, Norwich, West Haven, Meriden, Bristol, New London, Torrington, Willimantic and Derby also embraced professional teams at various times.

In the summer of 2008, two members of the Double-A Eastern League could be found in Connecticut: the New Britain Rock Cats, a Minnesota Twins' farm club, and the Norwich-based Connecticut Defenders, who are affiliated with the San Francisco Giants. Bridgeport was in its eleventh season as home to the Bluefish, who play in the independent Atlantic League.

GEHRIG AND OTHER STARS SHINE

Some of the game's most lionized heroes played for Connecticut minor league teams on the way up or, in a few instances, on the way down. Lou Gehrig was just twenty-one years old, barely removed from the Columbia University campus, when he batted .369 with thirty-seven home runs for the Hartford Senators of the Eastern League in 1924.

A current slugging first baseman of note, Todd Helton, wore the New Haven Ravens uniform for most of the 1996 Eastern League season, batting .332 in ninety-three games. That's just about his lifetime batting average with the Colorado Rockies.

One year later, David "Big Papi" Ortiz, of the Boston Red Sox, played for the New Britain Rock Cats. Record books show he was an authoritative .322 hitter in sixty-nine games with the Twins' farm club.

Still another first baseman of note, Norwalk native Mo Vaughn, made his professional debut with the then–New Britain Red Sox in 1989, hitting .278 in seventy-three games. The following season, the Boston-born, Killingworth-raised Jeff Bagwell batted a robust .333 for New Britain

The Waterbury Brasscos, managed by Kitty Bransfield, won their second straight Eastern League pennant in 1925. *Courtesy of the collection of the Mattatuck Museum, Waterbury, Connecticut.*

as a third baseman. Traded to the Houston Astros for a long-forgotten pitcher named Lary Andersen, Bagwell would amass 449 home runs and a lifetime .297 average as the Astros' first baseman.

Wade Boggs, whose 3,010 career hits and .328 average would lead to his Hall of Fame induction in 2005, played two seasons for New Britain, 1978–79, batting .311 and .325.

Another Hall of Famer, Warren Spahn, whose 363 victories are the most by any left-hander in the game's history, spent a productive 1942 season with the Hartford Chiefs of the Eastern League. Just twenty-one years old, Spahnie won seventeen games and compiled a 1.90 earned run average with the Boston Braves' farm club.

Joe Cronin, one of the game's hardest-hitting shortstops and a 1956 Hall of Fame inductee, batted .320 for the 1924 New Haven Profs in the Eastern League.

When the Waterbury Brasscos won the first of two consecutive Eastern League titles in 1924, one of their most noteworthy pitchers was "General" Alvin Crowder. The right-handed Crowder won 167 games in the American League and appeared in three straight World Series (1933–35) with the Washington Senators and Detroit Tigers.

Fred Lynn made his professional debut with the Bristol Red Sox of the Eastern League in 1973, forming a potent one-two punch with Jim Rice. Both would reach the heights with the Boston Red Sox two years later. *Courtesy of the* Waterbury Republican/*Tom Kabelka.*

In more recent years, Fred Lynn and Jim Rice composed the heart of the batting order for the 1973 Bristol Red Sox. Lynn, in fact, made the quantum leap that summer from the Southern California campus to the Double-A Eastern League without missing a beat.

Neighboring Waterbury had its share of stars-in-the-making during this period, too. Bobby Bonds played the outfield for the Waterbury Giants in 1967, forming a friendship with a much-loved local sandlot coach named Jim Spann that would endure until Spann's death some two decades later. "He's always been like a second father to me. He's always been a man I could talk to," Bonds said of Spann in a 1980 interview.

The Pittsburgh Pirates shifted their Double-A farm club to Waterbury in 1970, and pennant-starved Waterbury fans embraced this club when it rallied from a slow start to tie the Reading Phillies for the league lead at season's end. The Pirates then won the title with a winner-take-all, 3–2 playoff victory at Reading. This championship Waterbury team, managed by John "Red" Davis, was led by the slugging of left fielder Richie Zisk, who topped the league with thirty-four home runs, and twenty-year-old pitcher Bruce Kison. Both would become first-rate major leaguers.

Some of Kison's teammates called him "Sweetie," in deference to his beardless, boyish looks and angular six-foot, four-inch frame, but Bruce was a tough customer on the mound. He backed down against no hitter,

Dave Parker batted just .228 with the Waterbury Pirates in 1971 and was demoted to Class A Monroe in June. He would go on to win a pair of batting titles and a Most Valuable Player Award with the Pittsburgh Pirates. *Courtesy of the* Waterbury Republican/*Tom Kabelka.*

even Reading's massive first baseman, Greg Luzinski. The last of Kison's ten victories (against four losses) was achieved in the playoff against Luzinski's Phillies.

The Pirates were supplanted by the Waterbury Dodgers in 1973, and they would endure in the Brass City for four seasons. The 1976 season brought two future Dodger stars, Rick Sutcliffe and Pedro Guerrero, to Waterbury's Municipal Stadium.

The six-foot, seven-inch tall Sutcliffe pitched well on most occasions but was forced to settle for a 10–11 won-lost record. Still, most observers believed he possessed the skills and temperament to succeed. He did. Big Rick won the National League Rookie of the Year Award in 1979; with the Chicago Cubs in 1985, he captured the Cy Young Award on the strength of a 16–1 record.

Guerrero, a nineteen-year-old from the diamond mine that is the Dominican Republic, was placed at first base. He lashed base hits to all fields and finished with a .305 average. Five years later, Pedro socked two home runs in the World Series to help Los Angeles upend the favored Yankees in six games. He would conclude his fine major league career, mostly with the Dodgers and St. Louis Cardinals, with a dead-on .300 average.

Waterbury teams won no other championships in the following years, but several big-leaguers-in-the-making wore their uniforms. Among the most notable were Danny Tartabull (1982 Reds), Eric Davis (1983 Reds), Wally Joyner (1984 Angels), Cory Snyder (1985 Indians) and Jay Bell, who played shortstop for both the 1985 and 1986 Indians.

HARTFORD, A BASEBALL STRONGHOLD

With the exception of four seasons during the Depression years of the 1930s, Hartford was a minor league stronghold throughout the first half of the twentieth century. Capitol city teams won pennants in 1909, 1913, 1915, 1923, 1931 and 1944.

In the book by baseball historians Bill Weiss and Marshall Wright, *The 100 Greatest Minor League Baseball Teams of the 20th Century*, Hartford's 1931 Senators (97–40) are ranked twenty-sixth, and the 1944 Hartford Laurels (99–38) are ninety-ninth.

The 1931 club, managed by twenty-seven-year-old Charley Moore, who was also the backup catcher, dominated the Eastern League with its pitching, placing five among the league's top six earned run average qualifiers. The youngest of the quintet, twenty-year-old Van Lingle Mungo, would achieve fame with mediocre Brooklyn Dodgers teams. From 1932 to 1936, he averaged sixteen wins a season, leading the National League with 238 strikeouts the latter year.

Among the 1931 Senators' regular players, catcher Paul Richards would enjoy considerable success in the major leagues as a player, innovative manager, general manager and vice president. Playing with the Detroit Tigers, he was named the catcher on the *Sporting News*'s 1945 Major League All-Star Team.

With so many players serving in the armed forces and working in war-related industry during World War II, professional baseball teams had to scramble for talent. The 1944 Laurels (managed by former first baseman Del Bissonette) came up with enough skillful graybeards and younger men who also worked in defense plants to field a championship team. In fact, their .733 winning percentage was the highest in league history.

The Laurels' pitching leader, a bespectacled twenty-nine-year-old left-hander named Peter Naktenis, had a full-time job in the Colt firearms

plant in Hartford. He also complained of a sore arm each time he pitched. Limited to just twenty starting assignments, Naktenis completed all but one in accumulating an 18–3 record and a league-leading 1.93 earned run average.

Alas, no minor league team has called Hartford home since the 1952 season.

On July 26, 2008, a plaque was placed at the site of the old Hartford Base Ball Grounds. One of the original eight National League fields, it featured a covered wooden grandstand, fence, pressbox, clubhouses for both teams and a seating capacity of four thousand. The plaque at the site reads: "Dedicated to the City of Hartford and the men who played here and shaped the early history of our national pastime."

ENTER WEISS IN NEW HAVEN

The Elm City, as New Haven is known, also prospered in professional baseball during the game's early years. New Haven clubs won no fewer than eight league titles in a span of thirty-eight seasons (1890–1928).

George Weiss, born in New Haven in 1894, purchased the city's Eastern League club in 1919 for the borrowed sum of $5,000. He was just twenty-four years old. Weiss wasn't athletic enough to compete in baseball at New Haven High School (the forerunner of Hillhouse), but he earned a letter as student manager. Among the team's stars were Joe (later "Jumping Joe") Dugan and future Harvard football luminaries Charlie Brickley and Eddie Mahan.

Weiss operated the city's Eastern League team, known as the Profs, for a decade, winning pennants in 1920, 1922 and 1928. Not long afterward, the Yankees hired him to build a farm system, which he did with skill; at one point, the system fielded twenty-one clubs.

Promoted to general manager following the 1947 World Series, Weiss orchestrated signings and trades that would keep the Yankees on top for years. The team won an unprecedented five straight world championships (1949–53) and two more world titles, in 1956 and 1958. The club also garnered American League pennants in 1955, 1957 and 1960.

In 1971, George Martin Weiss was elected to the Baseball Hall of Fame by the Committee on Veterans. He died in a Greenwich, Connecticut nursing home on August 13, 1972, at the age of seventy-eight.

Branford native Frank "Beauty" McGowan was just eighteen years old when he joined
George Weiss's New Haven club in 1920. The Profs won the Eastern League title
and McGowan, an outfielder, went on to spend portions of five seasons in the major
leagues. *Courtesy of Frank McGowan.*

After the collapse of the original Eastern League in 1932, the New Haven area went through a forty-year period without professional baseball. West Haven entered the league in 1972, following its acquisition of the New York Yankees' Double-A franchise from Manchester, New Hampshire. The Yankees were an immediate hit, winning the league's American Division and then the pennant behind Manager Bobby Cox. Not too many years later, the latter would distinguish himself as the field leader for the Atlanta Braves.

The club's home field, Quigley Stadium, was a decaying wooden structure that became a deterrent to attendance, with the notable exception of that first year (102,537). Case in point: the 1976 West Haven Yankees, managed by Pete Ward, also won the pennant, but were witnessed by just 28,331 fans at home. The West Haven club repeated as champions in 1977 and 1979, but the increase in attendance was modest.

The Oakland Athletics shifted their Double-A franchise to West Haven in 1980. The West Haven A's won an Eastern League title in 1982, but then were uprooted and transferred to Albany-Colonie, New York, for the 1983 season.

When pro ball returned to the New Haven area in 1994, there was a new venue—historic Yale Field—and the Colorado Rockies were supplying the players. The New Haven Ravens drew large crowds for eleven seasons with such notables as Helton, infielder Craig Counsell (1994), pitcher Juan Acevedo (1994) and Bridgeport-born outfielder Angel Echevarria (1994–95) wearing Raven uniforms.

Yale Field had been the scene of the memorable pitching duel in the NCAA Tournament between Yale's Ron Darling and Frank Viola of St. John's on May 21, 1981. With an estimated fifty pro scouts among the crowd of three thousand looking on, Darling pitched a no-hitter for eleven innings, but lost in the twelfth, one to nothing, on a single, an error and a double steal. Both Darling and Viola would pitch for world championship teams later in the decade.

WATERBURY ON THE SCENE FIRST

Tucked away in the hills of the Naugatuck Valley, Waterbury once was the brass capital of the nation (hence its nickname, Brass City). Its minor league teams date back to 1884—earlier than most Connecticut communities.

Playing the Game

In fact, the first professional championship to be won in the Nutmeg State probably took place in the Brass City. The 1884 Waterbury Base Ball Club captured the Connecticut League title with a record of 34–13.

One of the game's true pioneers, Moses Fleetwood Walker, played for Waterbury teams in 1886–88. Earlier, Walker had become the first black to play in baseball's Major Leagues when he joined Toledo of the American Association in 1884, predating Jackie Robinson's arrival in Brooklyn by sixty-three years. Bigotry—not a lack of ability—forced Walker from the major league scene the following year, but he was able to continue playing in the minors for several years.

The second Waterbury club to win a championship was the 1910 squad managed by Mickey Finn. Consider this headline from page one of the *Waterbury Republican*'s September 10, 1910 issue: "WATERBURY WINS RAG OF GLORY IN SPECTACULAR WAY." In contemporary terms, the Waterbury professional baseball team won the championship of the Connecticut League.

The text was similarly flowery:

> *"Doc" Hayes and about 7,000 other fans saw the Waterbury baseball team tackle the Bridgeport aggregation at Reidville yesterday, witness the awful slaughter of the visitors and watched the Finnegans, figuratively speaking, grab the 1910 pennant, which has threatened to float out of their grasp. Not content with winning, the Finnegans rubbed it in on the Mechanics and left the field by the one-sided score of 12 to 5.*

Waterbury teams managed by a former major league first baseman named Kitty Bransfield dominated the Eastern League in the mid-1920s, winning back-to-back titles in 1924 (89–63) and 1925 (88–66). When the Brasscos franchise was transferred to Altoona, Pennsylvania, for the 1929 season, the professional game disappeared from the Brass City for nearly two decades.

The postwar boom following World War II led to the formation of the Colonial League, a Class-B grouping that included teams in Waterbury, Bridgeport, Stamford and Bristol. The Waterbury Timers finished first during the league's inaugural 1947 season, but lost to Stamford in the postseason playoffs.

The 1949 Timers were managed by Bert Shepard, a journeyman minor league pitcher who deserves a special place in the Baseball Hall of Fame. During World War II, Shepard's P-38 fighter was shot down by antiaircraft fire on May 21, 1944, and his badly injured right foot was amputated by a German surgeon. On August 4, 1945, wearing an artificial leg, Shepard became an inspiration for all World War II amputees when he pitched for the Washington Senators in a game against the Boston Red Sox. He even struck out the first batter he faced, George "Catfish" Metkovich.

The Shepard line for that heartwarming occasion read: 5.1 innings, three hits, one walk, two strikeouts, one run allowed.

Three weeks later, during a Senators-Yankees doubleheader, General Omar Bradley, General Jacob Devers and Assistant Secretary of War Robert Patterson presented Shepard the Distinguished Flying Cross and Air Medal in a ceremony held at home plate.

O'ROURKE LEADS EARLY BRIDGEPORT TEAMS

Among the state's cities and smaller communities that have a lengthy association with professional baseball, Bridgeport has won the fewest championships—just two across fifty seasons. This is not to suggest that the Park City is trying any less hard than its counterparts elsewhere.

After his career in the major leagues ended, "Orator Jim" O'Rourke returned to his hometown and became the owner, as well as manager and part-time player, of the Bridgeport Orators of the Connecticut League from 1899 to 1909. One of his sons, James "Queenie" O'Rourke, played for the Orators prior to joining the New York Highlanders in 1908.

The 1904 Orators won the league pennant with a 71–45 record, just ahead of runner-up Springfield (69–46) and third-place New Haven (69–47). O'Rourke, although fifty-two years old, was spry enough to appear in sixty-five games as a catcher, committing just seven errors and batting .286.

The biased writing of the period jumps off the pages of *Spalding's Official Base Ball Guide* for 1905. In his summation of the 1904 Connecticut League season, Dick Howell, the "sporting editor" of the *Bridgeport Herald* and *Waterbury Herald*, wrote:

> *It was during this exciting time that one of the great weaknesses of the league was brought vividly to mind—the incompetent umpires...The other umpires in the league, for the most part, lacked the moral courage to stand pat on positions of justice through fear of the players' threats.*

Playing the Game

After the collapse of the Eastern League during the 1932 season, the Park City endured a baseball drought (save for the Bridgeport Bees of the Interstate League in 1941) until the end of World War II.

In 1947, a Bridgeport restaurateur, Carl Brunetto, collaborated with a local athlete, Bobby Sherwood, to form the Bridgeport Bees of the Class-B Colonial League. They oversaw the construction of a new park, Candlelite Stadium, in the city's North End.

Sherwood, who had played football at Holy Cross prior to four years of army service during World War II, batted .300 or better in each of his three seasons and led Colonial League outfielders with twenty-three assists in 1947.

Baseball offered promise, but the Brunetto-Sherwood partnership reaped its profits from stock car racing, demolition derbies, boxing and "the night Tony Galento fought a bear." In the fall of 1950, a touring team of major league all-stars, including future Hall of Famers Warren Spahn and Johnny Mize, also proved fruitful at the box office.

"We made money on midget auto racing and we'd pour it into baseball," Sherwood said in a 1994 interview. "We used to pack 'em in."

Bridgeport would endure nearly half a century without professional baseball, until an enterprising local group led by Mary-Jane Foster, Jack McGregor and Mickey Herbert formed the Bridgeport Bluefish. The Bluefish began play in the independent Atlantic League in 1998, with home games in the new 5,300-seat Ballpark at Harbor Yard.

The managerial appointment of Willie Upshaw—the former American League first baseman who resides in nearby Fairfield—brought immediate recognition to the team and led to early success. Upshaw's second club brought the Park City its second baseball championship in 1999.

A WORD ABOUT NEW LONDON

Only one other Connecticut city may be found in the list of the top one hundred minor league teams compiled by Messrs. Weiss and Wright. That would be the 1916 New London Planters, who were awarded the fifty-seventh position. The Planters assembled an 86–34 record en route to winning the Eastern League pennant.

CHAPTER 2

ONE MAN'S ALL-TIME CONNECTICUT TEAM

It is presumptuous to select an all-star baseball team composed of men who were born in Connecticut. How does one accurately measure the accomplishments of the 176 native sons who played Major League Baseball since the formation of the National League in 1876?

While the game's rules have remained basically unchanged through the years, the equipment has evolved from primitive to expansive, ballparks have shrunken in size and night ball and jet lag are conditions unfamiliar to the athlete of decades ago. Today's player is infinitely larger and stronger than his counterpart of even thirty years ago, never mind the handlebar-mustachioed gentleman of the nineteenth century.

And yet, a mythical all-time team from the state seems worthwhile. This select group of athletes connects the dots of different generations and eras, and it gives younger fans an appreciation of ballplayers from an earlier time. It may also stimulate an argument or two. Feel free to disagree.

And so to proceed. In the infield, Norwalk native Mo Vaughn (1991–2003) holds down first base on the All-Connecticut Team. At his best, the economy-sized Vaughn was the dominant player in the American League, as indicated by his Most Valuable Player selection with the Boston Red Sox in 1995. That was the season Mo batted .300, walloped thirty-nine home runs and shared the league's runs batted in lead with 126.

Remarkably consistent in the American League, Vaughn put together six seasons with more than one hundred RBIs, six straight years

Mo Vaughn. *1996 Topps.*

with thirty or more homers and five consecutive seasons with .300-plus batting averages. Because of injuries and excessive weight, his career came to a premature end at age thirty-five, when he retired from the 2003 New York Mets. Still, Vaughn concluded with 328 career homers—more than any other native Nutmegger—and a sound .293 lifetime average.

The only serious competition at first comes from Walt Dropo, the six-foot-five, 220-pound first baseman from tiny Moosup. No state native ever had a finer freshman season than Dropo in 1950. That's when he tied Red Sox teammate Vern Stephens for the league's RBI title with 144, hammered thirty-four homers and batted .322. Yes, Big Walt was voted Rookie of the Year.

Less productive thereafter, Dropo nonetheless had some fine moments, notably in the summer of 1952, when, playing for the Detroit Tigers, he equaled Pinky Higgins's major league record for consecutive hits, with twelve. Walt completed his thirteen-year career with 152 homers and a .270 average.

There is a logjam at second base, with Farmington's Dick McAuliffe (1960–75) and a pair of New Haven natives, Hod Ford (1919–33) and Tommy Corcoran (1890–1907) as the principal candidates. McAuliffe is my choice. The Hartford native was an integral part of strong Tiger clubs throughout the 1960s and contributed a home run to the team's World Championship victory over the Cardinals in 1968. He finished with 197 homers and a .247 average.

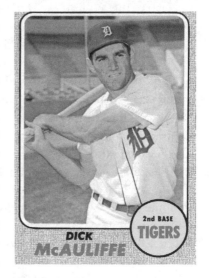

Dick McAuliffe. *1968 Topps.*

Jack Barry. *1911 American Tobacco. Courtesy of the Library of Congress, Prints and Photographs Division.*

Shortstop belongs to Meriden native Jack Barry (1908–19), perhaps the least known of the Philadelphia Athletics' renowned $100,000 infield, which featured second baseman Eddie Collins, third baseman "Home Run" Baker and first baseman Stuffy McInnis. Both Collins and Baker were inducted into the Hall of Fame, but Barry's superb defensive capabilities were an important ingredient to the A's winning four American League pennants (1910–11, 1913–14) in a five-season span. The club prevailed in the World Series in all but the latter year as well. Traded to the Red Sox in 1915, Barry contributed to a fifth flag that year as a second baseman.

After concluding his playing career with a .243 average, Barry returned to his alma mater, Holy Cross, as head coach. He coached the Crusaders for forty seasons, amassing a marvelous 616–150–6 won-lost-tied record and a .802 winning percentage—the highest among all Division I college coaches. Barry's 1952 Holy Cross squad won the NCAA championship.

Third base on this mythical all-star team goes to Tim Teufel (1983–93), the most recent of five Greenwich natives to reach the majors. Although he spent the bulk of his career at second base, he did participate in ninety-nine games at third. Teufel's .254 lifetime average packed some sting, as evidenced by a pair of seasons with fourteen home runs and a career total of eighty-six. He became the third Nutmeg State native (McAuliffe and Manchester's Jay Johnstone preceded him) to homer in the World Series when he

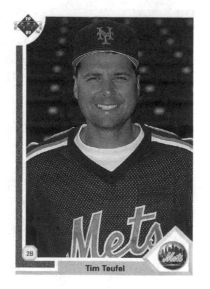

Tim Teufel. *1991 Upper Deck.*

connected off Bruce Hurst of the Red Sox in the fifth game of the 1986 classic.

In the outfield, one of the game's greatest defensive players, Waterbury's Jimmy Piersall (1950, 1952–67), is the hands-down choice as the center fielder. He is flanked by an earlier Waterburian, Johnny Moore (1928, 1932–37, 1945), and Hall of Famer "Orator Jim" O'Rourke (1876–93, 1904), who was born and raised in Bridgeport.

Piersall, whose battle with mental illness was recounted in the book and movie, *Fear Strikes Out*, captivated American League fans with his acrobatic catches for Boston, Washington, Cleveland and California. Twice he was awarded the Gold Glove (1958 and 1961). He was a pesty hitter, too, capable of a .322 average (1960) at his peak. He concluded his career with a .272 average and 104 home runs.

Moore, who grew up in the Waterville section of Waterbury, was an authoritative .307 hitter with the Chicago Cubs, Cincinnati Reds and Philadelphia Phillies in the 1930s. Consistent at the plate, he produced averages of .330, .323, .328 and .319 from 1934 to '37. On July 22, 1936, Moore thumped three home runs in a game against the Pittsburgh Pirates.

Few recall that Moore was a footnote in one of the game's most famous World Series moments: he was playing center field for the Cubs when Babe Ruth hit his "Called Shot"

Top: Jimmy Piersall. *1958 Topps.*
Middle: Johnny Moore. *Courtesy of the National Baseball Hall of Fame Library, Cooperstown, New York.*
Bottom: Orator Jim O'Rourke. *1887–90 Old Judge Cigarettes. Courtesy of the Library of Congress, Prints and Photographs Division.*

home run in the fifth inning of the third game in the 1932 classic at Wrigley Field.

O'Rourke's skills were so well-rounded that he appeared at all nine positions during his nineteen-year career in the National League. He starred with Boston, Providence (yes, Providence), Buffalo (yes, Buffalo), New York and Washington, eleven times batting .300 or better. This son of Irish immigrants had the distinction of getting the first hit in National League history; 2,303 more were to follow, and he finished with a .310 lifetime batting average. He was elected to the Hall of Fame, posthumously, in 1945.

Brad Ausmus. *1996 Topps.*

An educated man in an era when the sport was populated by drunkards and ruffians, O'Rourke earned a degree from the Yale Law School and opened a law practice in his native Bridgeport. He also served his native city as fire commissioner.

The all-star catcher on this mythical team is the still-active Brad Ausmus of the Houston Astros. The New Haven–born, Cheshire-reared Ausmus has won three Gold Glove awards (2001, 2002, 2006) and was an American League All-Star in 1999. As a hitter, he has been far more productive than his lifetime .252 average suggests.

The runner-up behind the plate? Brook Fordyce (1995–2004) of New London is the choice. He was a solid receiver and a career .258 hitter with five teams.

For a designated hitter on this all-Connecticut team, one man stands above the others—literally. That would be six-foot-three, 230-pound Roger Connor of Waterbury, the home run king of the Dead Ball Era, who was elected to the Baseball Hall of Fame by the Veterans Committee in 1976.

Roger Connor. *1887–90 Old Judge Cigarettes. Courtesy of the Library of Congress, Prints and Photographs Division.*

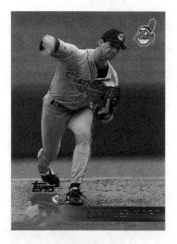

When he wrapped up his eighteen-year playing career in 1897, Connor departed as the game's all-time home run king (138), as well as its career leader in triples (233). Ruth surpassed Connor's home run record in 1921, and hundreds more have followed, but Roger still ranks fifth all-time in three-base hits.

A slugging first baseman for most of his days, Connor was a lifetime .317 hitter who enjoyed twelve seasons above .300. He became just the sixth player to wallop three home runs in a game (May 9, 1888) and he once collected six hits in as many at-bats (June 1, 1895).

The pitchers on this all-time team are drawn from the modern era—Fairfield's Charles Nagy (1990–2003), Canaan's Steve Blass (1964, 1966–74) and Southington's Rob Dibble (1988–93, 1995).

One can make a case for two pitchers from the nineteenth century, New Haven's William "Wild Bill" Hutchison and Waterbury's Francis "Red" Donahue, but they toiled in an era when the game was primitive and pitching staffs consisted of a handful of men. Hutchison won 184 games (versus 163 losses), all in the nineteenth century, while Donahue put together a 166–175 record in a career that spanned from 1893 to 1906.

For three seasons (1890–92), the five-foot-nine Hutchison was a workhorse with few equals, winning forty-two, forty-four and thirty-seven games and pitching 603, 581

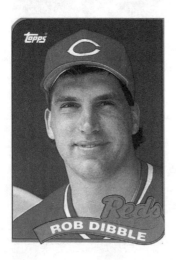

Top: Charles Nagy. *1996 Topps.*
Middle: Steve Blass. *1970 Topps.*
Bottom: Rob Dibble. *1989 Topps.*

and 627 innings with Chicago of the National League. He led the league in all of those categories.

Since the arrival of the twentieth century, Nagy has won more games than any other Connecticut-born pitcher—129 against 105 losses. For five seasons, he was the most consistent starter on strong Cleveland Indian teams, compiling records of 16–6, 17–5, 15–11, 15–10 and 17–11 from 1995 through '99. He appeared in two World Series, three American League Championship Series and two All-Star Games in that span.

Blass, who grew up in tiny Canaan in the Northwest corner of the state, assembled a 103–76 record, all with the Pittsburgh Pirates. The pitching star of the 1971 World Series, he won two games from the heavily favored Baltimore Orioles, capped by a four-hit, 2–1 victory in the decisive seventh contest.

Blass's finest seasons were 1972 (19–8) and 1968 (18–6); he topped the National League in the latter year with a .750 winning percentage. He pitched a league-high five shutouts in 1971, when his record was 15–8. Steve was just thirty-one years old when his career inexplicably went down the tube; he was unable to throw—or think—the ball over the plate. He has remained in the game as a broadcaster with the Pirates.

For relief, the Bridgeport-born, Southington-reared Dibble was a master with the Reds in the late 1980s and early '90s. He recorded all but one of his eighty-nine saves in a five-year span, and won twenty-seven games in all. Dibble reached his pinnacle in postseason play. He made four appearances against the Bonds-Bonilla Pirates in the 1990 National League Championship Series, striking out ten and allowing nary a run in five innings. He shared the playoff MVP award with fellow reliever and teammate Randy Myers.

In the 1990 World Series, Dibble pitched two scoreless innings of relief to earn the victory in Cincinnati's 5–4, ten-inning decision over the Oakland Athletics in the second game. The Reds went on to sweep the Series.

Edward "Ned" Hanlon, who was born in the eastern Connecticut town of Montville in 1857, is the lone Nutmeg State native to be inducted into the Hall of Fame for his managerial accomplishments. This earns him the manager's role on this mythical all-star team.

Hanlon was regarded as an innovative strategist who employed the hit-and-run and other revolutionary tactics. He won five National League pennants at the turn of the century, three straight with the rowdy Baltimore Orioles (1894–95–96) and two more with the Brooklyn Dodgers (1899, 1900). Three of his players—John McGraw, Hughie

Above left: George Weiss. *Courtesy of the National Baseball Hall of Fame Library, Cooperstown, New York.*

Above right: Morgan Bulkeley. *Courtesy of the National Baseball Hall of Fame Library, Cooperstown, New York.*

Left: Ned Hanlon. *1887–90 Old Judge Cigarettes. Courtesy of the Library of Congress, Prints and Photographs Division.*

One Man's All-Time Connecticut Team

Jennings and Wilbert Robinson—adopted much of his philosophy and became successful managers in their own right.

Hanlon, whose twenty-year record was 1,313–1,164 (.530), was elected to the Hall of Fame by the Veterans Committee in 1996.

Bobby Valentine deserves mention in the managerial category. The Stamford native put together an impressive resume as manager of the New York Mets, highlighted by a National League pennant in 2000, and he enjoyed some earlier success as manager of the Texas Rangers. His fifteen-year record stands at 1,117–1,072 (.510).

In 2003, Valentine left Major League Baseball to become manager of the Chiba Lotte Marines in Japan. He reportedly earns more than $2 million a year in the Land of the Rising Sun.

A word about Valentine's athletic prowess: although his major league playing career was aborted by injuries, his accomplishments in football and baseball at Stamford's Rippowam High School and in baseball's minor leagues were such that he was voted Connecticut's eighth Best Athlete of the Twentieth Century in *Sports Illustrated*'s poll.

Two other Connecticut natives are enshrined in the game's Hall of Fame. Morgan G. Bulkeley of East Haddam, who served as president of the National League in its inaugural year (1876), was inducted into the Hall of Fame in 1937. New Haven native George Weiss, general manager of the New York Yankees and architect of the team's post–World War II dynasty, was elected in 1971.

Which state native will be next to join them in Cooperstown? The reader is welcome to fill in the blanks.

ALL-TIME CONNECTICUT BASEBALL TEAM
Selected by Don Harrison, Summer 2007

POS.	PLAYER	HOMETOWN	YEARS	CREDENTIALS
1B	Mo Vaughn	Norwalk	1991–03	.293, 328 HR
2B	Dick McAuliffe	Farmington	1960–75	.247, 197 HR
SS	Jack Barry	Meriden	1908–19	.243, 5 World Series
3B	Tim Teufel	Greenwich	1983–93	.254, 86 HR
OF	Jimmy Piersall	Waterbury	1950, '52–67	.272, 104 HR

Pos.	Player	Hometown	Years	Credentials
OF	Johnny Moore	Waterville	1928, '32–37, '45	.307, 73 HR
OF	*Orator Jim O'Rourke	Bridgeport	1876–93, '04	.310, 2,304 hits
C	**Brad Ausmus**	**Cheshire**	**1993–**	**.252, 76 HR**
DH	*Roger Connor	Waterbury	1880–97	.317, 138 HR
P	Steve Blass	Canaan	1964, '66–74	103–76 W-L
P	Charles Nagy	Fairfield	1990–2003	129–105 W-L
RP	Rob Dibble	Southington	1988–93, '95	27–25 W-L, 89 saves
Mgr.	*Edward "Ned" Hanlon	Montville	1889–1907	Won 5 NL pennants

*Baseball Hall of Fame
Bold indicates active in 2008

CHAPTER 3

INTERVIEWS WITH TWENTY-FIVE OF THE NUTMEG STATE'S BEST

SIMPLY BELLA: LIFETIME GREENWICH NATIVE REACHED TOP WITH YANKEES, ATHLETICS IN 1950s

Some would suggest that Zeke Bella was unlucky. He hit .300 everywhere he played, but he was in the talent-rich New York Yankees farm system, and outfielders named Mantle, Bauer and Slaughter were wearing pinstripes in New York. In the 1950s, the Yankees ruled baseball (nothing new there), and only a select few reached the top. Bella did, but not for long.

But you will hear no complaints from this soon-to-be-seventy-four-year-old Cos Cob resident. "Few people get a chance to realize their dream. I got to play in the major leagues," Bella said during a recent interview. "I enjoyed it. I met a lot of good people. There were only sixteen teams then. If I was coming up now, and you have 360 more ballplayers…"

The words end, but his meaning is clear. If John "Zeke" Bella were a rookie today, he would be hitting line drives in Yankee Stadium instead of in the high minors.

Bella, a compactly built five-foot-eleven, 185-pounder in his heyday, spent more than seven seasons in professional baseball, but his time in the American League was limited to fifty-two games spread over two summers. Five appearances with the pennant-winning 1957 Yankees.

Forty-seven games with the lackluster Kansas City Athletics in 1959. A .196 lifetime batting average. That was it.

If he harbors any resentment, it's toward his manager in Kansas City—Harry Craft.

"I didn't get a shot (with the Athletics)," he said without bitterness. "When you're a rookie, it's not easy to pinch hit in the majors." Bella was competing for playing time in an outfield with Roger Maris—just a year removed from stardom with the Yankees—Bob Cerv, Bill Tuttle and Russ Snyder.

His memories of that season are vivid. He recalls a situation in Cleveland, with the flamethrowing Herb Score on the mound. "We're losing 2–0 in the top of the ninth, and he sends me up to pinch hit for Joe DeMastri. Bases loaded, two out. I doubled off (Herb) Score and we win, 3–2."

Bella's only American League home run came on August 13, 1959, against the Orioles' Jack Harshman, who had become a decent left-handed pitcher after failing as a first baseman. "Hoyt Wilhelm pitched a three-hitter against us the next day, and I got two of the hits," he recalled. "So I'm four for seven in two games."

Despite that productivity, Craft elected to bench the right-hand-hitting Bella the next night against the Yankees, though they were pitching ace left-hander Whitey Ford.

"Cerv liked to hit against Ford so he got to play," Bella recalled. "The next day I'm batting fourth against Bob Turley."

They didn't call Turley "Bullet Bob" for nothing. He shut down Bella and his Kansas City teammates. Zeke concluded the 1959 season with seventeen hits in eighty-two at-bats, a .207 batting average, and vanished from the majors. He was just twenty-nine years old.

"I had two eye operations, the left eye. I couldn't see the ball *good* anymore," said Bella, whose career average in the minor leagues was a superb .335.

Zeke Bella is one of Greenwich's finest all-around athletes. Born in Byram to the late John and Anna Belicka, he went on to star in three sports at Greenwich High School (GHS). (His visage appears under "Most Athletic" in the 1947 *Compass* yearbook.) As a senior, he quarterbacked the 1946 Cardinals to a seamless 9–0 football season, which culminated in the school being awarded its first Waskowitz Trophy as state champion. He was a high-scoring guard on the GHS basketball team and a combination outfielder–first baseman; he sometimes pitched on the diamond.

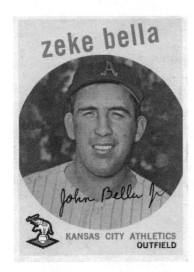

Zeke Bella. *1959 Topps.*

Although a natural right-hander, he threw with his left arm—which merits an explanation. "We were at church, and I fell down cement steps and broke my right arm. They set it wrong, and I started to throw lefty."

Bella's football prowess was such that Princeton offered him a scholarship, but he would have required a year of prep school to get his academic credentials in order. Instead, he went to work at Fawcett Publications and played semipro ball in North Carolina and Nova Scotia for a couple of summers. "I was making twenty-five dollars a week at Fawcett. They gave me seventy-five dollars a week to play ball in Hertford, North Carolina."

The Yankees took note of his quick bat and signed him to a professional contract in 1950. He received a $500 signing bonus, with the stipulation that he would get an additional $500 if he lasted the 1951 season.

No problem. Bella broke in with a lusty .382 average in fifty-eight games with Amsterdam, New York, of the Class-C New York–Canadian League. Promoted to Binghamton of the Eastern League in late summer, he responded with a .317 average in twenty-one games.

He was on his way. Or was he?

This was the era of the Korean Conflict, and Bella received his draft notice. He spent the next two years in Uncle Sam's army, both stateside and in Stuttgart, Germany, before emerging as a private first class and resuming his baseball career.

"I was glad to serve," he said, simply. "I don't hold that against anyone."

Rejoining Binghamton, Bella overwhelmed Eastern League pitchers in the summer of 1955. In fact, he won the batting title with a robust .371 average and outdistanced everybody, including a pair of stars in the making. Maris, then a young outfielder with Reading, hit .289. Bill Mazeroski, who would become a Hall of Fame second baseman with Pittsburgh, batted .293 for Williamsport.

The executives in the Yankee farm system were paying attention now. With Triple-A Denver, Bella hit .320 in 1956 and .317 in 1957, earning a promotion to New York in the latter season. Believe it or not, that elevation cost him some money.

He chuckles at the memory.

> *They brought me up September 1, which meant I wasn't eligible for the [World] Series. Our Denver team won forty-six out of forty-nine games to end up a few games out of first place [in the American Association] and went on to play in the Little World Series. The Yankees voted me a quarter share from the World Series—only $900. Each share in the Little World Series was worth $1,900. That promotion cost me a thousand bucks.*

Yankee Manager Casey Stengel employed Bella in five September games, resulting in ten at-bats and one lone hit, a single "off Willard Nixon of the Red Sox." Nixon was a serviceable pitcher with mediocre Red Sox clubs throughout the decade.

During his brief stay with New York, Bella relished the opportunity to study Mantle, who would hit .365 that summer, and Boston's Ted Williams, who won the fifth of his six batting titles with a .388 average.

"There's the greatest hitter that ever lived," Bella said of Williams. "Joe DiMaggio was probably the best all-round ballplayer I ever saw."

In 1958, Bella's bat contained enough hits for a .339 average with Denver, but there was no return to Yankee Stadium. On September 29, 1958, his contract was sold to Kansas City. Two years later, his eyesight impaired, he was out of baseball.

Bella returned to Greenwich and became a full-time letter carrier with the U.S. Postal Service. He and his wife, Lorraine (née Cortellini), a registered nurse, settled in Cos Cob and raised three daughters, Mary (Glascock), Diane and Cathy (Korman). The family circle now embraces five grandchildren.

Long retired from the post office, he continues to work part time as a driver for Toyota of Greenwich. If a particular model is needed at a dealership in, say, New Jersey, he will bring it there and return in a different vehicle.

Zeke and his bride of forty-six years spend winters in their condo at Tequesta, Florida, a community located near Jupiter on the Sunshine State's eastern seaboard. Another Greenwich native who happened to play Major League Baseball lives nearby—Tim Teufel.

Bella, who survived a bout with colon cancer two years ago, laughs at baseball's current salary structure, where the average wage for a major league season is in the $1.8 million range. "I made the minimum, $6,000," he said. "I couldn't live on that in Greenwich."

The minimum annual salary for today's first-year player is $300,000. "I could," he said, "live in Greenwich on that today."

Rather well, one presumes.

Greenwich Citizen, July 23, 2004.

BLASS DAY: CANAAN PAYS TRIBUTE TO A SON

CANAAN—"They could put me in a box tomorrow and I wouldn't feel I've been cut short."

This was Steve Blass, a deeply moved Steve Blass, responding Friday to a crowd of some four thousand in Railroad Plaza who came to honor the Pittsburgh Pirates' World Series pitching star on "Steve Blass Day."

The homecoming celebration for Falls Village's—and Connecticut's—favorite son was held at the historic Canaan Railroad Station, which was draped in red, white and blue bunting for the occasion.

Blass, his wife, Karen, and their sons—David, seven, and Chris, five—sat on the platform with other family members and invited guests as speaker after speaker lavished praise on Steven Robert Blass, athlete, citizen and man.

"He's the best spokesman we have for the school and the area," said master of ceremonies Ed Kirby, who was Steve's baseball coach at Housatonic Regional High School in Falls Village. Kirby, like Blass, has prospered with the times; he's the school's principal now.

Admittedly nervous, the twenty-nine-year-old Blass maintained both his poise and sense of humor. "If I had been this nervous in Baltimore," he cracked, "I'd have thrown the first seven pitches back to the screen."

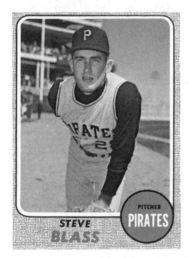

Steve Blass. *1968 Topps.*

43

Pitching in a World Series, said the Pirates right-hander who twice tamed the supposedly invincible Baltimore Orioles to give Pittsburgh its first world championship since 1960, is "the most exciting, most fantastic thing I've ever been through. It's all I thought it was when I was six years old."

The town of Canaan, in which Falls Village is located, wore its festive best. American flags and similarly colored bunting decorated buildings in the center of town. Blass's likeness, on drawings and in photos, was hung everywhere.

"Collins Diner Welcomes Steve," proclaimed the sign atop the diner opposite the railroad station. Other businesses did the same.

Stores closed early and many did not open at all. Blass's alma mater was dismissed at 12:30 p.m., and the elementary schools in the six-town district closed forty-five minutes later.

Groups of youngsters attired in full baseball uniforms (in the football season, no less) surrounded the station platform, seeking autographs and perhaps some pitching tips. Spectators jammed the station plaza, while others watched from a hill on the opposite side of Main Street.

The fall beauty of the Canaan countryside provided the perfect backdrop for what Blass called "a finer day than last Sunday."

Last Sunday? That was D-Day in the World Series, when Blass baffled the Orioles, 2–1, on four hits in the decisive seventh game.

Speakers included U.S. Senator Lowell P. Weicker, Lieutenant Governor T. Clark Hull, U.S. Representative Ella Grasso, state Senator Edmund Power of Torrington, Commissioner of Consumer Protection Barbara Dunn and state Representative Gordon Veill of Goshen.

Hull read a message from Governor Thomas J. Meskill, who was out of state. Weicker went him one better, though, by presenting Blass an autographed photo of President Nixon.

Other speakers included William P. "Hank" O'Donnell, sports director of the *Waterbury Republican-American*; Hartford sportscaster Bob Steele; the Reverend Robert F. Keating, pastor of St. Jude's Church in Derby; Ron Dower, who was the first baseman on Blass's high school team; and Bob Whalen, the Pirate scout who signed him.

In addition to his World Series exploits, Steve also was honored as the Little League's most distinguished graduate for 1971. Morgan Schafer, president of the Canaan Little League, presented the pitcher an engraved silver tray for "helping us get back on our feet."

Blass had purchased newspaper ads and also made a personal appeal to others to help the league, which was in danger of folding. The league has survived.

Several times Kirby injected humor into the proceedings, once by presenting Bob Blass, Steve's father, an "Oscar for your TV performance during the third game of the World Series." The senior Blass, it can be recalled, leaped onto the roof of the Pirates dugout and was nearly clobbered by Three Rivers Stadium security personnel when he attempted to reach his son, who had just pitched the Pirates back into the Series with a three-hit, 5–1 triumph.

Singer Bing Crosby, who happens to be a Pirate vice president, sent Blass a congratulatory telegram, which Kirby read aloud. Other telegraphs were received from Baltimore shortstop Mark Belanger and syndicated sports columnist Jim Murray, who likewise is a Canaan native.

Blass, who dined with the Falls Village selectmen at noon, rode into town in an eighteen-car motorcade. He was seated in an open car shaded by a top resembling a Pirate baseball cap.

Canaan had seen nothing like this before. Reporters were present from the New York dailies, the Boston papers and virtually every Connecticut newspaper. Several radio and television stations were on the scene, too.

Further evidence of the event's importance was the appearance of several vendors who regularly work the Yale Bowl and the New Haven Arena. They reported a brisk business in Pittsburgh banners and Steve Blass buttons.

Later, at a press conference held in the courtroom at the town hall, Blass revealed that he and his wife—who, incidentally, is the sister of Pirate relief pitcher John Lamb—planned to maintain their home here. They had been seeking a residence with the hope of providing a more routine existence for their sons.

"But we realized that we didn't want to leave this part of the country," said Blass, who was seated on the judge's bench.

Asked if he planned to hit the banquet trail this winter, baseball's man of the hour replied, "I don't want to get into the banquet and appearance thing too heavily. I want to have time to work out, as I did last year."

He expects to receive some endorsements and has, he said, "sent out an item myself to Dr. Pepper."

Although the telephone in the Blass household has been ringing incessantly—"at least 96 calls," he said—they decided against changing their number, at least for a few weeks, because "most of the calls will be from people we want to hear from."

When the day ended, Ross Grannan, one of the event's organizers, said, "Everything went just fine." He was so right.

Waterbury Republican, October 23, 1971.

NO SPOT FOR BOISCLAIR

ST. PETERSBURG, Florida—Bruce Boisclair is a Connecticut Yankee in King M. Donald Grant's court. The twenty-four-year-old outfielder might be the least known of the Nutmeg State natives who have reached baseball's Major Leagues in recent years. He could, if the Mets' faith is rewarded, turn out to be the best.

As spring training 1977 winds down, Boisclair (pronounced "Bo-clare") finds himself as the number four outfielder on the club managed by Joe Frazier. After an eventful rookie season in which his .287 batting average was exceeded by just two regulars, Joe Torre and Ed Kranepool, the former Danielson resident isn't completely satisfied with his station.

"I'd like to be given a chance to start," Boisclair declared. "I don't think they opened up the positions enough. It would make for a better camp if there was competition for jobs. Guys who have the good camp should get to play."

Bruce Boisclair. *1980 Topps.*

The Mets, who are feeling box office pressure from the Yankees (Shea Stadium attendance was at an all-time low in 1976, and the projection for the current season is even more distressing), can't be totally fair.

Dave Kingman, as the club's principal everyday drawing card and its most lethal long-ball hitter, is assured of a place in the outfield. John Milner, the renowned "Hammer" and the only other proven power hitter, will be out there, too, when he isn't sharing first base.

Interviews with Twenty-five of the Nutmeg State's Best

Frazier has turned over center field to Lee Mazzilli, a twenty-two-year-old switch-hitter from Brooklyn who makes basket catches à la Willie Mays. While his big-league dossier shows just twenty-four games (and a .195 batting average), his flair for the dramatic and potential sock at the gate stand him in good stead.

The six-foot-two, 190-pound Boisclair doesn't hit the ball out of the park—he had just two home runs in 286 at-bats with the Mets a year ago and just sixteen in five and a half major league seasons—and he isn't spectacular, but he can do a lot of things.

He can catch fly balls (he had just three errors all season) and he can steal bases. He is a left-handed hitter who can hit left-handed pitching (he's ten for thirty-two, averaging .313) and bunt (he's had six sacrifices and twelve hits in this manner). Based on recent performances, he also hits with some degree of consistency.

The Boisclair spring average, up to and including Friday's 2–1, thirteen-inning victory over the Red Sox, was a sound .290. More importantly, he says, "I've been hitting the ball real *good* and I'm very satisfied with that. It's given me a lot of confidence. Last spring I think I had two hits and hit .118. The big thing is to make good contact."

Bruce's bat might have been even more productive this spring, but he hasn't been completely up to par since experiencing "stomach problems" in Venezuela while playing winter ball. The problems resurfaced as dysentery during the Mets' recent trip to the Dominican Republic. He missed three games in all.

Boisclair realizes that the club's refusal to venture into the free-agent market was a boon to the younger players in camp. He disclosed that Grant, the Mets' chairman of the board, "spoke to me" and "said it was a great opportunity for me. I think the pitchers, Seaver and Koosman, wanted to see the team go out and buy some players. I hope they don't go down with the older players. It's smart if they're trying to rebuild."

Although his parents retired two years ago to St. Petersburg, a convenient location for them to watch their son in spring training, Bruce Armand Boisclair still feels close to Connecticut. Born in Putnam, he was raised in Danielson, in the state's eastern corner, and attended Killingly High School, "which had just over a thousand students then."

In the late 1960s, Boisclair was Killingly's most illustrious athlete, an all-state football player at tight end, a basketball player of some note and, of course, a much-honored outfielder.

Scheduled "to go to BC on a football scholarship," he opted instead for an offer from the Mets, who selected him twentieth in the June 1970 free-agent draft. He progressed slowly through the Mets' farm system, spending nearly three seasons with Triple-A Tidewater before getting his chance in New York last season.

There wasn't a better pinch-hitter in a Mets uniform than Boisclair, who went to the plate twenty-one times in these emergency situations and came away with twelve hits and a startling .571 average.

This year, he'd just as soon play every day and leave pinch-hitting to Kranepool, Torre and the other veterans.

Waterbury Republican, March 27, 1977.

BEFORE TEUFEL THERE WAS CASTIGLIONE

In the late 1940s and early '50s, Major League Baseball was a far more exclusive club than it is today. There were just sixteen teams—none west of the Mississippi—and four hundred players.

Greenwich-born Pete Castiglione was one of the select four hundred, a five-foot-eleven, 175-pound infielder who played with mediocre Pittsburgh Pirates teams in that era. Teammate Ralph Kiner hit home runs by the carload, but Pirate pitchers stopped nobody.

"We could score runs, but our pitching staff was terrible. We couldn't get anybody out," Castiglione recalled in a recent telephone interview.

Peter Paul Castiglione celebrated his eighty-first birthday in February, and he celebrates life on a daily basis with Joan, his wife of fifty-four years, in Pompano Beach, Florida. They have been blessed with two children (Sharon and Peter III, who lives in the same community) and five grandchildren. His mind remains keen and he is fit enough to play tennis several times a week.

Although Pittsburgh was a chronic second-division club, Castiglione savors the years he spent in a Pirate uniform. He was a versatile infielder and an adequate hitter, capable enough to bat .268 and .261, respectively, as the club's regular third baseman in 1949 and '51. He also filled in at shortstop and second base. Across 545 games with the Pirates and Cardinals (1947–54), the Castiglione batting average was an acceptable .255—or one percentage point higher than that of Tim Teufel, another son of Greenwich who became a major league infielder in the 1980s.

Pete Castiglione. *1952 Bowman.*

"Bing Crosby was one of the Pirates' owners, and we'd see him quite a bit in spring training (in San Bernardino, California)," Castiglione said. "Every year he'd have a big party for us before we'd go back east to start the season. Groucho Marx and a lot of other stars would be there."

Castiglione remembers Kiner, the seven-time home run champion and Hall of Fame outfielder, as "a regular guy" who was "good with everybody" on the club. "I saw him a few years ago at an exhibition game here (in Pompano) and chatted with him a bit."

Joe Garagiola, the catcher who became a noted wit and sports announcer, was traded to the Pirates in 1950. Castiglione found his new teammate to be "a pleasing guy, but not the wisecracker he became in later years."

Like dozens of other ballplayers in that era, Castiglione lost three of his prime years to World War II. Enlisting in the navy following the 1942 season with Harrisburg, Pennsylvania, of the Inter-State League, he found himself serving as a radioman aboard a destroyer escort and then a fleet tanker in the Pacific.

Did he see action? And how. He was there for the invasions of the Solomon Islands and Okinawa. "I remember the kamikazes. The Japanese were losing the war, and they were sending their airplanes into our ships."

Castiglione resumed his playing career in 1946. He batted a career-high .342 with Selma of the Class-B Southeast League and the next year moved up to Triple-A Indianapolis, where he hit .270 and, more importantly, met a local girl, Joan Murdock. They were married the day after Christmas 1947.

Castiglione's most productive day at bat took place late in the 1951 season and proved costly to the Brooklyn Dodgers, whose seemingly insurmountable thirteen-and-a-half game lead was being chipped away by the onrushing New York Giants. "I had two home runs and a couple more hits against (Don) Newcombe, and we beat 'em in Brooklyn," he said. "That was a big game."

On another occasion, Castiglione came within an eyelash of history by participating in two triple plays in one game. It happened against the

Chicago Cubs. In what would have been the day's second triple play, "the umpire called the runner safe at first, but I think we had him."

Traded to the Cardinals in June 1953, Castiglione slipped from the majors the next season, but played five more years in the Triple-A International League. In "retirement," he worked as a letter carrier in Florida for more than thirty-five years.

Although Castiglione left Connecticut in the late 1940s—he last visited Greenwich in 1989 for his fiftieth high school reunion—memories of his hometown remain crystal clear. He was the youngest of five children born to Peter and Margaret Castiglione, and the family lived above his father's grocery store on Davis Avenue.

Despite the Depression, the senior Castiglione was a trusting proprietor. He allowed customers to charge items and, as Pete recalled, "gave them the benefit of the doubt."

"It was a great town to grow up in," he said. "There were some big estates in the northern sections of town, but it wasn't like it is now. My grandfather came from Italy and we were one of the first Italian families in Greenwich."

At Greenwich High, young Pete was the goalie on the ice hockey team and handled shortstop for the Cardinal baseball team coached by J.B. Conlon. He also played summer ball for the Majestics, "the town champions."

After graduating from high school in 1939, Castiglione pursued his dream by attending the Joe Stripp Baseball School in Florida, where he impressed instructor Jimmy Jordan, a part-time Pirate scout. He signed with Pittsburgh for $100 a month and reported to Hutchinson, Kansas.

Ah, money. Castiglione never made much in baseball, with $13,000 being his peak salary with the Pirates. He did qualify for a baseball pension, though.

"I don't resent what the guys make today, but I think it's ridiculous—all sports—as far as money goes," Castiglione said. "The owners made the mistakes [by] giving players the big contracts, and they can only blame themselves. Heck, one of these guys makes more in one game than our whole [Pirate] organization made in a year."

That statement may not be an exaggeration. The "guy" in question, Alex Rodriquez of the Texas Rangers, earned $21 million this year, a princely sum that translates into $129,629.63 per game. Double wow.

Greenwich Citizen, October 4, 2002.

DAWLEY DREAMS OF REDS,
BUT HE'LL BE IN TRIPLE A

ST. PETERSBURG, Florida—There was a time when Bill Dawley, Connecticut born and bred, would have relished pitching in Waterbury.

Now isn't the time.

"I've had two years in Double A. I think I've proven myself," said the personable twenty-two-year-old right-hander from the eastern Connecticut community of Lisbon. "It would have been nice, near home. But I got to play in Nashville, where we drew a lot of people and won the pennant."

Bill Dawley is one of the bright pitching prospects in the Cincinnati organization, bright enough to be listed on the club's forty-man winter roster for the second straight year.

Two seasons in Nashville, where the Reds' Double-A club was based prior to its shift to Waterbury, have primed him for life in Triple-A Indianapolis. He knows that spring training is strictly a let's-see-what-he-can-do proposition.

"Everybody dreams," Dawley said, "but realistically, I can't see myself making the club this year. A few guys would have to get hurt for me to be there. There's no pressure on me at all. I'll stay here as long as possible and then go to Indianapolis. This year's going to be exciting."

Bill Dawley. *1987 Topps.*

Last year at Nashville was exciting, too. The Sounds, a nice blend of pitching, speed and hitting, won the Southern League title and played before nearly 500,000 fans at home—an astounding number on the Double-A level. Promotional nights were frequent—"They gave away seven used cars one night," Dawley recalled—but the fans responded to the excellent baseball as well.

Dawley's personal 1979 season began on a low note. "After fifty innings my ERA was like seven," he said. "I can't explain it, unless it was because I was disappointed at not going to Triple A. In the second half I turned myself around. My ERA was in the low two's and I wound up nine and nine. The strong finish got me on the major league roster again."

William Chester Dawley is a talkative sort, as friendly as he is large (six feet, five inches and 205 pounds). He considers himself fortunate to be paid to play a game.

"My father has been a milkman for twenty-five years. He gets up at 5:00 a.m. and works six days a week including Christmas and other holidays," Bill explained. "I worked with him this winter, so I got to see what it was about."

Robert Dawley, father and milkman, was scheduled to spend a portion of spring training with his son.

Bill was the Reds' seventh-round draft choice in June 1976, after a remarkable career at Griswold High School. Opposing batters never had a chance; four no-hitters and an assortment of low-hit games were some of his achievements. His high school batterymate, Roger LaFrancois, has done rather well himself, reaching the Triple-A level in the Red Sox organization.

Life after high school for Dawley has meant baseball and Karen. Bill and Karen Hyde were married in September 1976, after his first professional season in Billings, Montana. The transition from high school sweetheart to baseball wife seems to have taken. Their marriage, after three and a half years, is thriving, and Karen is enough of a fan to attend all of her husband's games, regardless of whether he's scheduled to pitch.

Bill's first appearance of the spring, against the world champion Pittsburgh Pirates, went well. One inning, no runs. He surrendered a double to Mike Easler, but retired three other Pirates on ground balls.

"Last year I was a little awed because it was the first time I faced major league hitters," he said. "Now I feel more confident. I believe I can pitch in the major leagues if given the chance. The Reds think I'm a prospect so I guess it's just a matter of time."

Waterbury fans probably won't see Bill Dawley in a Reds uniform— unless it's on a television screen.

Waterbury Republican, March 20, 1980.

EX-MAJOR LEAGUE PITCHER WARNS OF DRUG, ALCOHOL ABUSE

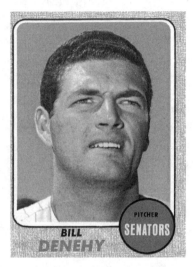

Bill Denehy. *1968 Topps.*

They drifted into the Pitt Center in twos and threes, many with backpacks in hand and backward baseball caps on head. For Sacred Heart University's student-athletes, Bill Denehy's appearance was a command performance, even if it was six o'clock on a Thursday evening and dinner awaited.

Few in the crowd of 450 had heard of Denehy, the ex–major league pitcher with a ninety-five-mile-an-hour fastball whose career was aborted by drug and alcohol abuse. But his message of failed dreams and his life as a recovering addict was powerful. He hoped he would touch the life of somebody in the audience.

"People ask what percentage of students do I save. I can't answer that," Denehy said. "I just hope to make an impression so they can make a few choices...the right choices."

As a young man and adult, Denehy made too many of the wrong choices, and they nearly ended his life. Excessive drinking and drug abuse cost him his pitching career, his marriage, his relationship with his daughter and his second career as a college baseball coach. And now, at fifty-three, he shares his travails, and his message of hope, with audiences throughout the country on college campuses, at business meetings, at treatment centers and on radio and television.

Alcohol abuse came early, when Denehy was a two-sport star at Middletown's Woodrow Wilson High School in the early 1960s. "I didn't drink much, but every time I drank, I got drunk," he said.

As a senior, he pitched Wilson to the Class B state title and then, spurning a basketball scholarship to St. Bonaventure University, signed a bonus contract with the New York Mets.

After two seasons in the minor leagues, Denehy was a National League rookie, a strapping six-foot-three right-hander who ranked just behind Tom Seaver—and ahead of other notable youngsters named Jerry Koosman and Nolan Ryan—on the Mets' 1967 roster. But booze was part of the baseball culture, as it is now, and that exacerbated his problem.

"My Triple-A manager, Solly Hemus, told us we couldn't leave the clubhouse until all the beer was gone," Denehy recalled.

An event that heralded the beginning of the end took place in a game against the San Francisco Giants on May 3. Some fifty thousand people were in the stands at Shea Stadium, and Juan Marichal was the opposing pitcher. On the surface, everything seemed fine.

Denehy reached back and threw the hardest pitch of his career in the direction of Willie Mays's head. "Willie went down and stayed down for a couple of minutes, checking his body parts," Denehy said. "What the fifty thousand people didn't know was that one hour earlier, I took a pill, a Black Beauty. The veteran pitcher who gave it to me told me it would make my fast ball three feet faster. It did."

What Denehy didn't realize was that in his quest to increase his velocity, he had torn muscles in his pitching arm. Never again would he throw as hard.

At the end of the 1967 season, Denehy became the living answer to a trivia question: what pitcher was traded to the Washington Senators for a manager—Gil Hodges—who would lead the Mets to their first world championship?

A few years later, he drifted to the Detroit Tigers, where he was united with another alcoholic—the team's manager, Billy Martin. "There were no rules," Denehy said. "We could drink up until game time."

At age twenty-five, Denehy was an angry and resentful man. His drinking had increased and his self-esteem had collapsed. The pugnacious Martin took advantage of the situation by using him as a relief pitcher who would intimidate the opposition.

"He put me in a game to hit a batter. In four short years, I had become an assassin," said Denehy. "In one game, he wanted me to hit Vida Blue. I hit him in the kneecap…got him out of the game."

Two years later, a sore-armed Denehy was released by the Boston Red Sox. His career record: a dismal one win and ten defeats. He was out of baseball, a twenty-seven-year-old man without job skills.

In the mid-1980s, he resurfaced as the baseball coach at the University of Hartford to assemble a powerful team. He even out-recruited the University of Connecticut for a budding superstar named Jeff Bagwell. But Denehy's erratic behavior on the field, capped by a brawl-marred game against UConn, led to his dismissal midway through the 1987 season. The Hartford athletic director who fired him was the same athletic director who invited him to speak at Sacred Heart—Don Cook.

And then Denehy's life really went sour.

"Physically, I hit rock bottom on July 4, 1991," he said. "I was with three other people and we had three eight balls of cocaine and a bag of marijuana. My nose started to bleed profusely. I literally was wiping the blood away and taking another dip. I really got scared."

Fear drove him into rehab, and now nearly eight years have passed since Bill Denehy did drugs or drank alcohol. In sobriety, he has reconstructed his life, including reconciling with his daughters, one of whom, Heather, accompanied him to Sacred Heart last Thursday. And now he devotes his time to warning today's generation about the dangers of substance abuse.

"Physically, no question I belonged in the big leagues. But I had a real deep fear of failure and lacked the emotional stability to handle it," Denehy said. "What I'm doing now is as gratifying as anything I've been involved in."

Fairfield Citizen-News, April 2, 1999.

DIORIO: NOT THE END, A NEW BEGINNING

Ron Diorio is a former professional baseball pitcher. He's made it official. After ten seasons, 405 games, forty-seven victories, thirty-five defeats and sixty-five saves, the most genuine, level-headed athlete I've ever met has come to the realization that there is life after baseball.

"I don't consider this an end," he said this past week. "I look upon this as a new beginning."

The decision to "retire" was made with some reluctance. Ronald Michael Diorio still believes he can pitch, and pitch successfully, in the major leagues. A 2.37 earned run average across twenty-three games in the National League season of 1973 showed that he belonged.

Still, there were other considerations. Age (he'll be thirty-three). His wife's pregnancy (Joanne Diorio is expecting their first child in mid-May). A job with the Covino Real Estate Agency, and some other business possibilities as well.

"I don't want to stay in the game just to say I'm in it. I can do other things. I'm not totally reliant on the game," Diorio explained. "If I really

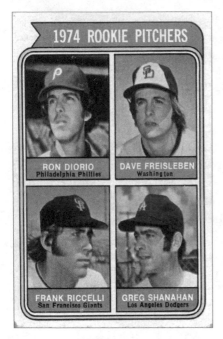

Ron Diorio. *1974 Topps.*

wanted to play, I would have written to twenty-six major league teams."

In fact, Ron Diorio did write to two teams, Toronto and Oakland, several weeks ago. Both have struggling pitching staffs; both decided to struggle without him.

There could have been a job in the minor leagues, though. Two weeks ago there was a long-distance call from Caracas, Venezuela. The Caracas team in the newly sanctioned Inter-American League was interested. Ron listened politely for a while, said "no thanks" and hung up.

Diorio has positive feelings about his decade in organized baseball. Oh, he has some regrets, but on the whole he considers himself fortunate to have been there. "The travel, the associations, the obvious benefits. I just couldn't have gotten this experience anyplace else," he said. "That's why I can leave it. I can take it for what it was."

The high point? No contest. "That was when I pitched in Shea Stadium on Labor Day 1973. The whole family was there, led by my father. All our lives he used to take us down there. That was my greatest experience."

That was the day Ron faced—and retired—eight straight Mets batters. He never got to face the ninth, wondrous Willie Mays. "I actually wouldn't have minded [Felix] Millan getting on to have faced Mays. That would have been some experience," he recalled.

God gave Ron Diorio size (he's nearly six feet, six inches tall) but not great physical ability. That he was able to progress from moderately successful high school pitcher at Sacred Heat to honorable mention all-American at the University of New Haven, and then to the major leagues, says something about the inner Diorio. The man worked and worked and worked to succeed.

And then, after a 24–1 record at New Haven ("a kid from Southeastern Massachusetts Institute threw a no-hitter and beat me, 2–0"), he refined his trade in baseball's minor leagues. From Walla Walla, Washington, to Newport News, Virginia, to Reading, Pennsylvania, and then, on August 8, 1973, to the road-gray uniform of the Philadelphia Phillies. Ohmigoodness.

He pitched in San Diego the following night, when Manager Danny Ozark summoned him to replace a chunky right-hander—fellow Waterburian Dave Wallace. Tell that to Ripley.

"From the Father Shea League to Sacred Heart to American Legion to New Haven College to the Carolina League to the big leagues to the same game…to me relieving him. That," Ron said with mock finality, "is a Guinness job right there. It's gotta be."

The Diorio of late summer 1973 was a revelation to the Phillies. He made twenty-three relief appearances for the team of Carlton, Luzinski and Bowa, finishing eleven games and receiving credit for one save. There wasn't a lower earned run average on the staff than Diorio's 2.37.

Ron's sidearm, right-handed pitches troubled some of baseball's finest right-handed hitters that year—George Foster ("I got him three, four times"), Ron Cey, Cleon Jones, Dave Cash. And, yes, even Jim Rice.

Rice, then a twenty-one-year-old wunderkind with Bristol of the Eastern League, paid Diorio a tribute he isn't about to forget. As Ron recalls, "Just before I went up from Reading, Jim came up to me and said, 'You can say you don't want to see me anymore and I don't want to see you anymore.' Well, I did have good luck with him."

If baseball is behind him, now and forever, Ron Diorio isn't about to turn his back on athletics as a whole. There aren't many better young basketball referees than the tall man with the mustache and thinning hair. His schedule this winter, a mixture of junior varsity, high school varsity and college games, is busy. Coaches and athletic directors respect his work.

"I truly enjoy it as much as I've enjoyed anything," he said. "It's a challenge. The hardest thing I've ever had to be consistent about. You have to start the game being perfect and you have to maintain it."

I shall miss Ron Diorio the pitcher. I imagine a lot of us will. Men of his caliber don't come along too often, in baseball or elsewhere. There is one bright consolation to his "retirement," though: he's home to stay.

Waterbury Republican, February 11, 1979.

DROPO'S KEY TO SUCCESS

The sovereign state of Connecticut has produced greater baseball players than Walt Dropo. Not a dugout full, but several. He falls short of Calvin Murphy, Johnny Egan or John Williamson on a basketball court and there may be dozens of football players who possessed more skill. Nick Pietrosante, Floyd Little and Bob Skoronski come immediately to mind. But for exhibiting proficiency in each of the so-called major sports, it's doubtful any one man could equal Walter Dropo, the Moose from Moosup.

Dropo, who celebrated his fifty-second birthday just the other day—time does not stand still, even for ex-athletes—will receive a long-overdue honor tonight. The former Boston Red Sox slugging star, along with Skoronski, who captained the great Vince Lombardi–coached Green Bay Packer teams, and golfer Dick Siderowf will be presented Gold Keys at the Connecticut Sports Writers' Alliance annual dinner in New Haven.

"As I understand it, we'll have two hundred or three hundred of our own friends, relatives at the dinner," Dropo said from his home in Marblehead, Massachusetts.

Walt and Elizabeth Dropo have been fixtures in this North Shore home for twenty-two years, residing in a comfortable English colonial. There are three Dropo children, daughters Carla, fourteen, and Tina, thirteen, and Jeff, their seventeen-year-old son, "who played offensive end in high school last fall. He's six-one, 190 and he's applied to UConn." Walt earns his keep these days with a Boston investment firm.

Walt Dropo. *1957 Topps*.

Dropo has no regrets about his choice of professional sports. An all-around athlete of rare ability at the University of Connecticut in the 1940s, the strapping six-foot-five, 220-pounder probably could have made the grade in pro football or pro basketball.

"I had reasonable success as a football player at Connecticut," he said. "I was better as a defensive end, although I played offense, too. I could go down and out, ten or fifteen yards, but I didn't have real speed."

The Chicago Bears were impressed enough to draft the UConn man—"I had a good talk with (George) Halas"—but he turned the Bears down.

On the basketball court, Dropo was a phenomenal scorer in an era when a 12-point scoring average was regarded as superior and a 15-point average was almost unheard of. For his entire varsity career at the state university—forty-one games separated by a stint in Uncle Sam's army during World War II—Walt averaged 20.7 points.

"I used the hook shot, the jump shot to get most of my points," recalled Dropo, a center during his collegiate days. "I think I scored thirty-five points a couple of times against Rhode Island. That's when Rhode Island was instituting the fast break with players like Ernie Calverley and Stan Stutz. Fellows weren't playing defense the way they do today."

The Boston Celtics were intrigued enough to contact Walt, and he frequently played against National Basketball Association stars in semipro games. But again, baseball won out. Neither Walt nor the Red Sox, who signed him in 1947 for a "reasonable bonus," ever regretted the decision.

He spent portions of thirteen seasons in the big leagues, from 1949 to 1961, appearing with the Detroit Tigers, Chicago White Sox and Cincinnati Reds, in addition to the Red Sox. Renowned as a power hitter, the big, right-hand-hitting first baseman walloped 152 home runs and compiled a respectable .270 batting average in 1,288 games.

Two feats stand out in Dropo's major league career—his fabulous rookie season with the Red Sox and the two-day span with Detroit in 1952, when he tied the major league record for consecutive hits.

What a rookie year. Promoted from Louisville in the early weeks of the 1950 season, Dropo launched a batting rampage that lasted the duration of the campaign. He averaged better than a run batted in a game, accumulating 144 in 136 games to tie teammate Vern Stephens for the American League lead.

He also finished on top with 326 total bases, while ranking among the leaders with thirty-four home runs, a .322 batting average and a .583 slugging percentage. Rookie of the Year? Who else?

Never again did Walt's bat destroy opposing pitchers in this fashion, although he remained a threat at the plate. "I think Fenway Park is conducive to that type of record," he said. "Stats are built on certain things. Fenway Park was ideal for me. You can't expect to match Ted Williams's stats. I think I had some talents, but I don't think I had running. I was gifted in a lot of other ways."

A key figure in a nine-player trade between Boston and Detroit in June 1952, Dropo really exploded for the Tigers on July 14 and 15, collecting twelve straight hits in three games to tie Pinky Higgins's record. Five came off four Yankee pitchers, including Vic Raschi, on the first day as Detroit romped by an 8–2 score. The next day, in Washington, Dropo rapped seven consecutive hits and eight overall in a doubleheader, although the Senators swept the last-place Tigers, 8–2 and 9–8.

"Lou Sleater stopped my streak," Walt remembered. "He got me out on a high fast ball and I popped it up. I was a little cautious."

Waterbury Republican, February 2, 1975.

ANGEL SOARS IN THREE SPORTS

In this age of the single-sport specialist, Angel Echevarria is a throwback to the era of Chip Hilton. Hilton, who sprang from the mind—and pen— of the late Clair Bee, was a fictional high school and college athlete who threw sixty-yard touchdowns passes, scored thirty points in basketball games and hit tape-measure home runs. He was a straight-A student and a straight-arrow young man.

Bee's series of Hilton books, published in hardcover by Groset & Dunlap, were popular among boys during the late 1940s and into the 1960s. Every youngster, or so it seemed, aspired to be Chip Hilton.

Angel Echevarria *is* Chip Hilton. With one major difference: he's real. He's genuine enough to catch touchdown passes for Bassick High School of Bridgeport; authentic enough and springy enough to pull down rebounds by the bushel; and real enough to bat .517 as a high school junior.

"He might be the best athlete in the state, along with Scott Burrell of Hamden," says a Bassick assistant coach named Bernie Lofton.

Mr. Lofton might be not overstating the case.

And Angel. What does Angel say about his remarkable proficiency in three sports? "I enjoy playing all of them, but I truly love baseball," he says.

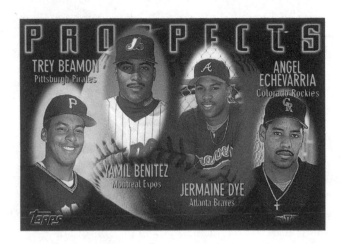

Angel Echevarria.
1996 Topps.

Baseball, say many people close to the Bassick scene, is the sport in which his future lies.

Angel Echevarria stands six feet, three and a half inches tall and his 180 pounds are spread across his angular frame. His words come out softly. He seems to have a feel for numbers; accounting and math are his strong suits in the classroom, where he has earned second honors.

He can recite batting averages, team won-lost records—even the number of yards in his touchdown receptions against city-rival Warren Harding High School the previous week. Score: Bassick thirty-four, Harding zero. He will also spell out the reasons for the Lions' bright 2–0 start in football, a welcome turnaround from the previous year's 2–8 record.

"This year, the team is working together. Nobody wants to be the star. It all comes down to playing together," says the Bassick senior. "We're not really big, but we've got a lot of heart."

Against Harding, several Lions distinguished themselves. Angel scored a pair of touchdowns on catches of twenty-two and thirteen yards, and he also blocked a punt. Kenny Garner, the sophomore quarterback, was responsible for both scoring passes, and he also ran for a score. A junior cornerback named Andre Younger and defensive end Cal Geer were thorns in the Presidents' sides throughout the game. Talented Dennis Moye and Dean Holliday exhibited superior running skills.

"Last year," says Bassick football coach Frank Brown, "we were basically a sophomore-freshman football team. We've matured to the point where we aren't making the young mistakes anymore."

Brown, like his counterparts in basketball (Harrison Taylor) and baseball (Jim Silvestri), is delighted to have Echevarria on his side.

Last year, he didn't. A commitment to baseball in the Pacheco League prevented Angel from wearing a Bassick football uniform last season.

"We have five players who play both ways, and Angel is one of them," explains Brown. "He has good hands and speed…And he's one of our co-captains."

Angel, who plays end on both offense and defense, shares the Bassick captaincy with Garner, Moye and tackle Fred Griffin.

On the basketball court, Angel Santos Echevarria makes most of his contributions as a rebounding forward. Last season he was instrumental in the Lions winning seventeen of twenty-three games.

"Due to his baseball skills, he has excellent anticipation on defense," says Taylor, who considers Angel one of the nicest young men he's ever met.

On the diamond, Echevarria really sparkled, both at bat and in right field. For example, he was voted the MBIAC's Most Valuable Player, the driving force behind Bassick winning the league championship with a 5–1 record (11–7 overall). He was also selected to the *New York Daily News*'s Fairfield County All-Star Team.

In eighteen games, he amassed thirty-one hits, including three home runs, two triples and five doubles, drove in twenty-two runs and struck out just three times. And, yes, he batted .517.

"In the American Legion World Series, they have a home run–hitting contest, and Angel and another boy from the Bridgeport Legion (Bassick teammate Ralph Gonzalez), made the final eight," Silvestri recalls. "Angel is more of a line-drive hitter, but he hit one ball—a real Dave Winfield–type line drive—that hit the top of the fence at Palmer Field."

It is ironic that Winfield is the athlete Echevarria most admires, although he is a rabid Mets fan. "Dave is my idol. They say I swing like him."

Echevarria's performance last spring was in marked contrast to earlier years, when, he says, "If I didn't hit a home run or a triple, I'd strike out." He credits his cousins, Angel and Santiago Llanos, both former Kolbe High School athletes, with providing the hitting discipline that transformed him into an athlete with pro potential.

"Both of them have pushed me," he says, "but Angel, he's the one who really told me to take a short step into the ball."

The growth is evident in Silvestri's eyes, too. "He's shown tremendous improvement from his sophomore year," says the Bassick coach. "He's willing to listen, which is half the battle."

Silvestri is much impressed, too, by Echevarria's .472 hitting and four home runs in Legion competition because "they're up against all-star teams."

And the future. Will Angel Echevarria sign a pro baseball contract after high school graduation, should that intriguing possibility present itself? The answer, at this stage, is no.

"I won't do that," he says, "because if something goes wrong, then you won't have anything to fall back on. I want to go to college."

Chip Hilton couldn't have said it any better.

My gut feeling about Angel was on target. Before his Bassick senior year ended, Echevarria's leadership and strong rebounding were important ingredients in the Lions' 23–0 basketball season, capped by a 76–72 double-overtime victory over Harding in the Class L state championship game at Central Connecticut State University in New Britain. On the diamond, Bassick produced its finest season in memory (17–4) as the Echevarria batting average soared to .536 and he was elected to the all-state team. He then enrolled at Rutgers University, where he became a three-time All-Atlantic-10 selection prior to his being drafted by the Colorado Rockies. He went on to appear in 328 major league games (1996–2002) and batted .280.

Bridgeport Light, October 12, 1988.

ELLIS IS TRYING TO WIN A JOB

FORT LAUDERDALE, Florida—There has been a change in command, but it doesn't figure to help John Ellis. His position on most nights will be bench. As in dugout. As in paid spectator. The husky thirty-two-year-old native of New London is offering no complaints, however, at least for public consumption.

"No, not particularly," he said, when asked if Don Zimmer's arrival as the Texas Rangers' manager would help his status. "Pat Putnam deserves a shot at first. He's just played so well this spring. And I don't think I'll catch again. Zim said, 'Just be alive.' If I make the club, I'll probably do some DHing against lefthanders."

If he makes the team?

"I haven't made the club yet," Ellis said evenly.

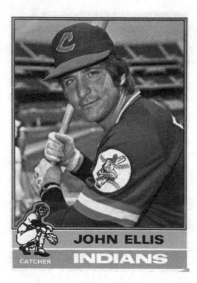

Johnny Ellis. *1976 Topps.*

John Charles Ellis made the all-injury club, though. Remember 1976? He was hitting .419 on May 9, and he had just helped the Rangers win eight straight games, when he slid into second base at Fenway Park. Disaster. A broken left leg and a dislocated ankle. End of season.

Last year, there was something called a traumatic neuritis in his right thumb. What it meant was that he had a severe bone bruise and couldn't grip the bat properly. He had just one home run in 182 at-bats and hit .236.

"I'd rather have a broken leg than have that thing," he said.

On the whole, though, Johnny Ellis has few complaints about his career in baseball. "I've played twelve or thirteen years. I've been injured a lot, but I've had my chances to play," he said. "When I've played, I've played pretty well."

True enough. There are 860 games in the Ellis dossier and a decent enough .264 average. Three seasons with the Yankees, three more with the Indians and now five with Texas.

When given the opportunity to play on a somewhat regular basis with Cleveland, he responded with a .270 average, fourteen homers and sixty-eight RBIs in 1973 and then .285, ten and sixty-four in 1974.

The Ellis who drove in sixty-one runs, clubbed twelve homers and averaged .285 in 316 at-bats with the Rangers in 1979 was a pretty tough out as well.

"It's a little late in my career to think about playing a full season again," he said. "I've fulfilled the role of platoon player for the last five or six years. I'm just satisfied to have a good summer job playing baseball."

Ellis can afford to look upon baseball as seasonal work. He's done well in business as president of John Ellis & Associates, a New London–based firm that specializes in land development. "We've had it for twelve years now. We have twelve staff members," he said.

Although John has spent most of his life in eastern Connecticut (he attended New London High and Mitchell Junior College and now calls East Lyme home), he has ties with the Naugatuck Valley. His parents,

Louis and Wanda Ellis, were raised in Ansonia. The senior Ellis made the Coast Guard a career "and was transferred around a lot."

After a desultory 1980 season, a season in which so much was expected and so little was achieved (76–85, fourth place), the Rangers' theme for 1981 is "Coming Alive." Ellis believes Zimmer, who succeeded Pat Corrales as manager last November 12, will help right some of the wrongs.

"Zim's real low-key, very knowledgeable. Everyone knows him as being dependable, somebody you can take at his word," he said. "We can be a contender this year, I really believe it. If the bullpen comes around, I think we have a chance of winning...going all the way."

The multi-player trade that brought Rick Honeycutt, a left-handed pitcher of skill if not of a winning record, from Seattle should be beneficial, too, he believes. Surrendering outfielder Richie Zisk in that transaction was regrettable, but necessary.

"Richie was a good player. He hit some home runs and he always drove in eighty runs," Ellis said. "But we've got other hitters, guys like Al Oliver and Buddy Bell and Mickey Rivers. Honeycutt should help our pitching."

John Ellis's .364 spring average (8–22) would seem to indicate he is capable of contributing to the Rangers' offense, too.

Waterbury Republican, April 1, 1981.

ON AND OFF THE FIELD, MEMORIES OF FORTY-THREE SUMMERS

Mickey Mantle's death this summer touched the lives of many in Connecticut, including former teammate Billy Gardner. Gardner, a trim, youthful sixty-eight, still lives in his native Waterford. He was a reserve infielder on the 1961 New York Yankees, one of the most powerful clubs in history. That was the season Mantle reached a personal peak with fifty-four home runs, although he finished second to his teammate Roger Maris, who hit sixty-one, breaking Babe Ruth's single-season record of sixty.

Mantle was a leader, Gardner said. "What I admire about him, he was always on the top step of the dugout getting the other guys

BILLY GARDNER   Minnesota
Second Base   Twins

Billy Gardner. *1961 Topps.*

going," rooting for teammates like Tony Kubek and Bobby Richardson. "I felt sad in August when he died," Gardner said. "I played with him, played against him. I was with him in recent years at a couple of card shows."

Gardner's career in professional baseball spanned two eras and forty-three summers, an uncommonly long period, as a player, coach and manager in the major leagues. For a decade (1954–63), he was the epitome of the "good-field, no-hit" infielder with the Yankees, New York Giants, Baltimore Orioles, Washington Senators, Minnesota Twins and Boston Red Sox.

Much later, after a dozen seasons as a minor league manager and several years as a coach, he managed in the American League. For nearly five seasons (1981–85), he led a youth-oriented Twins team, and then, for half a summer (1987), he managed the Kansas City Royals, succeeding Dick Howser, who had died of a brain tumor.

"I was fortunate to play with clubs in both leagues that won the World Series," Gardner said. "I even got to coach in the 1983 All-Star Game. Those were great days."

Gardner witnessed a lot of change during his travels. When he signed with the Giants' Bristol, Tennessee farm club as a scrawny seventeen-year-old in 1945, major league teams traveled by railroad and few players earned very much. Big-league baseball did not exist west of the Mississippi. When his career ended in August 1987, with his ouster as manager of the Royals, the game spanned the continent, clubs traveled by jet and the average major league salary was approaching seven figures.

If Billy Gardner wasn't a star, destiny placed him with those who were. Nine of his major league teammates—Mantle, Whitey Ford, Yogi Berra, Willie Mays, Hoyt Wilhelm, George Kell, Brooks Robinson, Harmon Killebrew and Carl Yastrzemski—are members of the Hall of Fame. He played with Mantle and Mays when both center fielders were at the top of their game.

"People always ask me to compare them, but it's tough," Gardner said. "Willie was a better outfielder, Mantle had more power. Both could do everything on a ball field."

It took Gardner a while to reach the National League—eight seasons in the Giants' minor league system and another year in the army. Some men might have quit, but he was a high school dropout, and he loved the game. He persevered.

"I worked at Electric Boat, a sub base. I unloaded cargo on the pier," he said. "Heck, I pumped gas during the winter even after I was in the big leagues."

He and his wife of forty-three years, Barbara Gardner, have three children, the youngest of whom, twenty-nine-year-old Bill Jr., played two seasons as an infielder in the Kansas City organization and made his managerial debut this summer with Butte, Montana, of the Pioneer League.

In 1954, the senior Gardner's persistence was rewarded when he joined the New York Giants, a team destined to win the pennant and sweep the Cleveland Indians in the World Series. He hit .213 across sixty-two games as a backup infielder and learned the game by observing the manager, Leo Durocher. Mays, twenty-three and just back from the army, won his only batting title, walloped forty-one home runs and was voted Most Valuable Player.

The Orioles acquired Gardner's contract in April 1956, giving him the opportunity to play second base regularly. For the next four seasons, he provided his new team with fine defensive play and timely, if infrequent, hitting. In 1957, his finest season, he hit .262, led the American League with thirty-six doubles and 644 at-bats and committed just twelve errors in 868 chances. His .986 fielding percentage topped all second basemen.

Gardner chuckled as he recalled an early incident in Baltimore. "Paul Richards, a soft-spoken guy and a good baseball man, was the manager," Gardner said. "We were playing Boston one night, and Ted Williams hit a ground ball that went through my legs, and we lost the game. Later, one of our coaches, Luman Harris, comes over and says, 'Richards wants me to hit you ground balls.' It's eleven at night, I say. 'Well, they left the lights on.'"

Dutifully, if reluctantly, Gardner returned to the field with Harris and scooped up grounder after grounder off the coach's bat.

Brooks Robinson was beginning his reign as the Orioles' nonpareil third baseman during those years, a Hall of Famer in the making. "You could see by his actions he was quick. Great hands," Gardner said. "He struggled at bat in those days. But then his bat speed picked up. The rest is history."

From June 9, 1956, through April 4, 1958, Gardner played in 361 consecutive games with Baltimore, an accomplishment in which he takes pride. The figure may appear modest in comparison to the records of Lou Gehrig and the modern Oriole, Cal Ripken Jr., but it ranks him fourth on the club's all-time list, behind Ripken, Robinson (463) and Eddie Murray (444).

"I'm not taking anything away from Gehrig, who was a first baseman," Gardner said. But he is more impressed that Ripken, a middle infielder, could play in this many games and not get hurt. "The Astroturf they play on these days," Gardner said. "One twist and you're out for a week."

Gardner played one more year, with the 1960 Washington Senators, and then—in a stroke of good fortune—was traded to the Yankees early the following season. If he was relegated to utility duty again, at least he had a front-row seat to watch Maris and Mantle's monumental home-run duel and the pitching artistry of Ford and Luis Arroyo.

The world champion 1961 Yankees won 109 games and hammered 240 home runs, a record that has yet to be surpassed. Gardner, dividing his time between second and third base, batted .212 and contributed one homer. In the World Series, he went to bat just once, lining out as a pinch-hitter in the ninth inning of the Cincinnati Reds' only win.

Those Yankees "were better, player for player, than the 1954 Giants," he said. "They were good guys, too. Whoever was together on the road went out together for dinner. I never saw any animosity between Mantle and Maris."

As an American League manager, there were to be no pennants for Gardner. He has the satisfaction of knowing he was responsible for molding the nucleus of young players—Kirby Pickett, Kent Hrbek, Mickey Hatcher, Gary Gaetti, Frank Viola—who were the backbone of the Twins' 1987 world championship team. Despite a second-place finish in 1954, he was released midway through the following year.

Gardner has warm memories of Puckett, the compactly built all-star outfielder who seems to possess Hall of Fame credentials. "When we brought him up from Toledo, he didn't even have money to pay for the cab ride from the airport, but he went four-for-five in his first game," said Gardner, who works as a part-time salesman for a meat company and is content to live with his baseball memories. "Kirby still gives me a call once in a while, when he comes to Boston."

New York Times, October 15, 1995.

KURT'S CAREER IS PEAKS AND VALLEY

DERBY—It is a warm Wednesday afternoon in July and Kurt Kepshire is seated at a table in Yellowtails, one of the more fashionable nightspots in this lower valley town. Why is the thirty-year-old right-handed pitcher blowing the froth off a cold one in a Derby, Connecticut pub when there are Pacific Coast League baseball games to be saved and a professional career at stake?

Because he is, as they say, between jobs.

The former Bridgeport Central High athlete was released by the Minnesota Twins' Portland, Oregon farm club a few weeks ago. The reason: a sore shoulder had rendered his pitching arm useless.

"It's frustrating. I tried to pitch with the pain but it wasn't working," he explains. "I was on the DL [disabled list] for twenty days. Now I'm a free agent."

Kurt Kepshire believes the injury occurred "on a cold day in Colorado Springs" when he threw too hard without sufficient warm-up. Whatever the case, he pitched infrequently thereafter, concluding with a 2–1 record for twenty-plus innings of work.

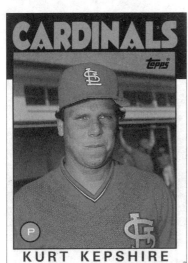

Kurt Kepshire. *1986 Topps.*

The Portland team physician advised him "not to throw for two months." Now he is seeking a second opinion from a local doctor, with the hope that this is merely an interruption to an eleven-year career, which includes sixteen National League victories, all achieved with the St. Louis Cardinals.

"I'm not done yet," he says, firmly. "If they don't see me pitching on television, I'll be down with the guys at Seaside Park. I can still pitch."

The fates are fickle. At this juncture four years ago, Kurt David Kepshire was in the starting rotation for a pennant-bound Cardinal team, right there with John Tudor, Joaquin Andujar and Danny Cox. He won ten games and lost nine.

On some occasions, National League hitters could do little more than wave feebly at ninety-one-mile-an-hour Kepshire fastballs. Recalls Kurt, "I was seven outs away from a perfect game against the Pirates. Johnny Ray broke it up with a bloop single. When Whitey (Herzog) took me out in the ninth inning, I got a standing ovation. That's something I'll always remember."

Coming on the heels of his 1984 rookie success—a 6–5 record and 3.30 earned run average enhanced by back-to-back shutouts against Montreal and Chicago, following his promotion in July from Triple-A Louisville—Kepshire seemed on the verge of becoming the toast of St. Louis.

Alas, it was not to be.

Admittedly, he didn't pitch well in the 1985 pennant drive. Tudor, who had a "career year," and some others did. When it came time to select the Cardinals' roster for the National League playoffs, Kepshire's name was omitted. It still rankles him today.

"You have to go with the hot players. I was cold," he admits. "I lost a little of my confidence in September. Being a power pitcher, I can't go to spots, I can't finesse people. I tried to throw more breaking balls in September, but I couldn't adjust."

What annoyed Kurt the most was the manner in which he learned of his deletion: from reading the *Chicago Tribune*. "At least be man enough to call me in the office," he says, placing the blame for the shoddy treatment squarely on the shoulders of General Manager Dal Maxvill. He doesn't fault Herzog, about whom he says, "I respect that man to no end."

So Kurt Kepshire, ten-game winner, was reduced to a spectator's role when the Cardinals defeated the Dodgers in the playoffs and lost to Kansas City in the World Series—after leading the Royals three to one in games.

A contract hassle with Maxvill in the winter of 1986 widened the rift between pitcher and general manager. Then, more puzzling doings. In his April debut, Kepshire dropped a 3–2 decision to Montreal, a game in which he permitted five hits in seven innings. "The next thing I know," he says, "I don't pitch for three weeks. Why didn't they trade me to a team that can use my services?" he wonders. "I wanted to be wanted."

Instead, the Cardinals demoted him to the minor leagues. Except for one subsequent inning of relief against Chicago that spring, Kepshire's activities have been confined to Triple A ever since—Louisville in 1986, the Mexico City Reds in 1987, Indianapolis and Portland in 1988 and Portland this season.

There were glimmers of hope, notably in Mexico, when "I must have thrown the best ball of my life." And there were low points, such as the unconditional releases he received from St. Louis and Cleveland, the latter following an abortive 1987 spring trial.

"I was home in Bridgeport, playing slow-pitch softball with my friends, when my agent told me about the chance to pitch in Mexico," Kurt relates. "He said it would be like a vacation." It wasn't; he pitched superbly.

Montreal, which had purchased Kepshire's contract from Mexico City, considered promoting him in the spring of '88 and again during the American Association season (in which he was eight and four with a 3.45 ERA for pennant-winning Indianapolis). Neither wish was fulfilled.

And now, here he is, at thirty, released for a third time. Will there be another opportunity?

"It hurts. I worked hard to get there. I sacrificed a lot of things," he says. "If I never make it back, at least I was there. I accomplished something I wanted to accomplish; I was successful."

For a moment, he recalls some of the people who provided early encouragement and support. Sumner Sochrin, Jim Dobbs and Tom Cianciola, his coaches at Central. "I take my hat off to those guys." And he speaks warmly of his father, Joe Kepshire, "who played catch with me all the time. There's a special bond between us."

Joe and Carol Kepshire consider Seymour home now, and Kurt has purchased a condo in Derby, but the dream began in Bridgeport.

His thoughts return to the present. "Cleveland called me the other day and offered me a job. They didn't know my arm situation. I can't tell you how much I appreciate that call. I'm hoping this [injury] is a minor thing. It's looking pretty good here. In September I want to begin a weight program for my shoulder."

The warm Wednesday afternoon is becoming evening. I wish Kurt Kepshire well as we part.

Bridgeport Light, July 26, 1989.

Joe Lahoud. *1973 Topps.*

LAHOUD: SURPRISE START

BOSTON—Carl Yastrzemski took the day off Wednesday. "It was just an ideal time to rest him," Red Sox Manager Eddie Kasko said.

Of course, the fact that a left-hander named Sam McDowell was pitching for Cleveland might have had something to do with it, too. Carl hasn't hit much lately, and the McDowell fastball has never been known to cure a batting slump.

In any event, Joe Lahoud was Carl Yastrzemski's replacement in left field Wednesday, although Sherm Feller, the Fenway Park public address announcer, wasn't informed of the change in the Boston batting order. He read off Yaz's name in the pregame lineups.

Unannounced, unheralded and under pressure to produce in a rare starting assignment, Lahoud soon made Feller, Sudden Sam McDowell and 17,153 Fenwayites aware of his presence. His leadoff home run in the seventh inning, a towering drive that hugged the right field line as if it were a long-lost relative, provided the Sox with a crisp 2–1 victory.

It was Joe's seventeenth American League homer—but his first against a left-hander. And such a left-hander.

"It was a fast ball," the twenty-four-year-old Danbury native explained afterward in the Boston clubhouse. He was leaning back on a stool in front of his locker. His audience consisted of a dozen or so newsmen, many of whom had journeyed over from his home state for Connecticut Sports Writers' Alliance Day.

"Sam," he said, "was throwing hard, but not as hard as the other night."

Lahoud saw McDowell for the first time on Monday night, in a game washed out by rain after three innings. Or, perhaps more correctly, Joe never saw him at all that evening. Sudden Sam struck him out. "He just threw the ball right by me. He's the hardest fast ball pitcher I ever faced," Lahoud said.

Yesterday was a different story, though. Joe, afraid of no one, even a flamethrower of McDowell's caliber, hung in there against the tall Cleveland left-hander. Neither the vaunted McDowell fastball nor the McDowell curve saw him bailing out.

On the subject of bailing out, McDowell reportedly said Joe wouldn't have hit the homer if he hadn't bailed out. Which brought this retort from Mr. Lahoud: "I give him credit as a pitcher. He should do the same for me as a batter."

Joe grounded out to short his first time up. Rather sharply. In the fourth, he drilled a one-bouncer to second that, if hit a few feet to either side, would have been a single. In the eighth, with two on and two out, he worked the count to three and two before looking at a third strike.

"It was inside," Joe said.

Afield, Lahoud handled three chances flawlessly, although his throw to second base, on Kurt Bevacqua's second-inning double, was on the weak side. "I just tried to throw the ball before I had it," he confessed.

Lahoud has been getting a few starting assignments in the past week. Sometimes it is a spur-of-the-moment thing. "Sometimes five or ten minutes before game time." Yesterday, Kasko gave Joe the word an hour before the game.

"Yaz came in and said his thumb was bothering him," Joe said. At least, though, he is getting the chance to play, not pinch-hit.

Joe, over-all, is batting .281, a power-packed .281. His eighteen hits include five homers and three doubles and have accounted for eleven RBIs. His slugging percentage is an impressive .563 (and isn't that the true test of a slugger?).

Project the Lahoud figures over a full season and he will hit forty-five homers. But will he be given the opportunity?

"I don't think I lost any ground out there today. It's kind of hard [for Kasko] with four outfielders doing an adequate job. He can only play three of us. He's been as fair as he can," the former Abbott Tech and University of New Haven athlete said.

Billy Conigliaro, the Red Sox outfield regular likely to lose out if Lahoud steps in, didn't lose any ground himself yesterday, either. He ripped two doubles (he leads the Sox with twenty) and a triple off McDowell, who allowed only five hits over-all and struck out fourteen (including George Scott and winning pitcher Ray Culp three times apiece).

"Everybody gets discouraged after a while," Lahoud continued. "A couple of times I wanted to go in and ask [Kasko]. But we were losing. I asked Yaz what to do. He said, 'Now isn't the time to ask him.'"

And what does Kasko say about the muscular six-foot, 198-pound Nutmegger who is so anxious to play regularly? "I'm just going to try to take advantage of both of them in the Baltimore series this weekend. It'll be Joe against the right-handers, Billy against the lefties."

No, Joe Lahoud, former pinch-hitter deluxe, didn't lose any ground at all yesterday.

Waterbury Republican, June 24, 1971.

A LAMB IN NAME ONLY

Ask John Lamb why he's stuck it out in baseball, despite Class A buses and Class A ballparks and Class A hotels, and you'll get a two-word answer: "I'm stubborn."

John Andrew Lamb of the Sharon, Connecticut Lambs is stubborn. And confident. Coming off his eleven-win, four-loss 1969 season with Pittsburgh farm Salem of the—yup—Class A Carolina League, he's a relief pitcher about ready to escape the bushes.

"I know I can do it—all I have to do is convince somebody else," he said via telephone from Clinton, Iowa, his off-season home for the third winter. It became his off-season home in November 1967, when he married Connie Hesler, a Clinton girl.

The former Housatonic Regional High School pitching star, one of very large names on the Connecticut schoolboy scene in 1965, has a baseball heritage to live up to. His brother-in-law is Steve Blass, a thirty-four-game winner with Pittsburgh the past two summers.

Tom Parsons, who pitched some for the Mets (pre-championship days) and more recently with Pittsfield of the Eastern League, is his cousin. An older brother, Pete Lamb, also spent some time in the Pirate organization as a pitcher. It's in the family.

Until this summer, John Lamb had done little to carry on the tradition. He won some, lost some and his five-year won-lost record for Class A and rookie leagues was an uninspiring 36–36. Many of his earned run averages, the true indication of a pitcher's worth, were on the high side, sometimes five plus.

Was John Lamb discouraged? Is John Lamb, at age twenty-three, discouraged? "No sir. I'm not quitting. I love the game."

If the first five years were often sour, everything turned up sweet in 1969. The Pirates made him a reliever, exclusively, and the six-foot-three, 180-pound right-hander responded with bear-down enthusiasm,

John Lamb. *Courtesy of the Pittsburgh Pirates.*

although "I didn't like it at the time. I didn't think I'd get to pitch enough."

When the Carolina League season ended in September, Lamb had pitched enough—if fifty appearances in a 140-game schedule can be regarded as enough. There was quality with the quantity: eighty-seven strikeouts, only thirty-five walks in ninety-seven innings and, easily most satisfying, a hard-to-see 1.95 ERA. Individually, it was a fine year, as it was from a team standpoint. Salem finished on top of its division.

"There were no easy situations—each time it was a test," said Lamb, summing up relief pitching.

From every standpoint, Lamb figures to move up the ladder, finally, come spring. He could wind up with the Waterbury Pirates, with whom he would appear before friends and family ("I never know who's in the park...even my wife, who hollers encouragement all the time").

If he comes through with an especially strong spring, John could move up to Columbus, which would simplify a lot of paperwork. He's currently on the International League club's roster.

In any event, Lamb feels he must move up. "I told [farm director] Pete Peterson I'm not going back to 'A'," he said with conviction, reasoning, "Why should I go back to a league I was eleven and four in?"

Why, indeed.

Until spring comes, John Lamb, husband first and pitcher second, will work a construction job. His company's current project is a power plant in Cordova, Illinois. John's an electrical clerk. (In the remote possibility that his baseball days are numbered, John is taking a correspondence course in electronics, but he doesn't care to talk about that.)

Lamb considers life in Clinton, Iowa, population thirty-three thousand, idyllic. Midwest. Good folks. Apple pie. Real America. He was pitching with Clinton, then a Pirate farm in the Midwest league, when he and Connie Hesler met in 1967.

Their first meeting was in, of all places, the Clinton ballpark, and they went to a party that night. "It was," said Lamb in one of his frequent atypical Now Generation statements, "love at first sight."

Waterbury Republican, December 14, 1969.

BASEBALL STAR THANKS HIS HOMETOWN

On the morning after Thanksgiving, about 250 people, from wide-eyed children to white-haired adults, surrendered an extra hour or two of sleep to gather in a small gymnasium at Fairfield High School. Many were armed with baseball cards bearing the picture of Charles Nagy, the all-star pitcher for the Cleveland Indians who was born in Bridgeport and raised in Fairfield.

For much of the morning, the broad-shouldered, soft-spoken Nagy fielded questions from the audience, then took a seat in another room to sign autographs and pose for photographs. In a brief ceremony, he presented an Indians cap and baseball glove to the school for its trophy case.

"I love to go out and talk to kids in schools and libraries," said Nagy, twenty-five years old. "That's what makes this so much fun."

This free appearance was scheduled as a thank-you to his community for its support through the years, he said. He had been invited to a dinner in January, at which Nagy would have become the first inductee into the Fairfield High School Hall of Fame. He couldn't make that date but arranged the November visit instead.

Fairfielders are understandably proud of Charles Nagy. In just two full seasons, he has developed into one of the American League's foremost pitchers, a right-hander capable of assembling a 17–10 won-lost record and 2.96 earned run average with a fourth-place Indian team. In a recent poll of major league managers, he was chosen as the league's number one pitching prospect.

Other examples of Nagy's prowess: he ranked among the league leaders in most major categories last year, including earned run average (seventh), strikeouts (eighth, with 169), innings (fourth, 252), complete games (tied for fourth, with 10) and shutouts (tied for fourth, with 3). His strikeout-walk ratio, 169–57, was also exceptional.

On August 8, Nagy reached the heights with a one-hit, 6–0 victory over the Baltimore Orioles. Only Glenn Davis's infield single, with one

Charles Nagy. *1998 Topps.*

out in the seventh inning, prevented Nagy from becoming the sixteenth Indian pitcher to throw a no-hitter. He also shut out the heavy-hitting Minnesota Twins, 5–0, and the New York Yankees, 3–0.

Selected to play in the 1992 All-Star Game, Nagy pitched one perfect inning against the National League and, to his own amazement, beat out an infield single—the first all-star hit by an American League pitcher since Ken McBride of the California Angels had one in 1963. "They were harassing me after the hit," he said with a sheepish grin. "The guys were joking about it."

Nagy seems unaffected by his success. Those who knew him when he was a three-sport athlete at Roger Ludlowe High (which was merged with Andrew Warde to become Fairfield High School) and the Big East pitcher of the year at the University of Connecticut say he is unchanged, still self-effacing and quietly confident. His "aw-shucks" demeanor is reminiscent of ballplayers from another, simpler time.

"It's hard to look back and see the things I've done," he said. "I'm just living out a dream. Baseball's a kid's game. I'm just a big kid playing baseball."

Ed Bengermino, Fairfield High's baseball coach and the man who coordinated the recent visit, has a vivid memory of Charles Nagy, high school pitcher. "I coached against him twice, and both times he didn't pitch," the coach said. "One time he played shortstop and went four for four with three home runs. It would have been better if he'd pitched."

James Conley, a longtime teacher in the Fairfield school system and a leader in the formation of the Hall of Fame, recalled some Nagy heroics in basketball. "I remember a game in Stamford when he threw a length-of-the-court pass to somebody who scored, and we won a game we weren't supposed to win," he said. Nagy also impressed fans as an all-state football player at Ludlowe.

Few men from Connecticut have exceeded Charles Nagy's accomplishments in Major League Baseball. In the past seventy years, only two native sons, Joey Jay of Middletown and Steve Blass of Canaan, have won more games in a season. Blass and Frank "Spec" Shea of Naugatuck were the only others to pitch in an all-star game.

Jay, who gained a measure of fame as the first graduate of the Little Leagues to reach the majors, enjoyed back-to-back twenty-one-victory seasons with the Cincinnati Reds (1961–62); Blass won eighteen games (1968) and then nineteen (1972) for the Pittsburgh Pirates.

Nagy said he hoped to join Blass, Shea, Rob Dibble of Southington and Gary Waslewski of Kensington as World Series participants. That might not be too far in the future, he said, if Cleveland continues its climb in the American League East.

"We can't rest on what we did last year," he said. "A lot of us are kicking ourselves for our slow start last year. We need a couple of more quality pitchers, and we can contend next year. We're only going to get better."

Nagy said his batterymate, catcher Sandy Alomar, was a "part of the nucleus of the great young talent we have." He included in that group two outfielders, Albert Belle (thirty-four home runs, 112 runs batted in) and Kenny Lofton, who led the league with sixty-six stolen bases as a rookie, and the second baseman, Carlos Baerga (.312 batting average, twenty homers, 105 RBIs).

During the question-and-answer session, a young fan wondered which all-star players Nagy would surround himself with if given the option. "I'd stick with the eight guys I have around me right now," he shot back.

All signs point to Charles Nagy remaining in Cleveland. He and his wife, Jackie, are building a home near the city. His contract with the club extends through the 1995 season, and he has been chosen as the team's player representative, which, because of his youth, can be viewed as a tribute to his maturity.

"You used to hear jokes about Cleveland being the armpit of the country," he said. "But they've really turned the city around. In 1994, our new park, which will look a lot like Camden Yards [the new ballpark in Baltimore], will open. I'm looking forward to that."

For an opening day pitcher in the new stadium, the Indians' manager, Mike Hargrove, need look no further than the soft-spoken man from Fairfield.

New York Times, December 13, 1992.

PITCHING MEMORIES WITH PHIL NASTU

Vin Scully's lyrical voice dominates the Nastu living room on this October evening. "The Dodgers, as has been their custom in these autumn games, are playing with emotion…" Phil Nastu smiles as the World Series drama unfolds on his television screen, as the Dodgers play David against the Oakland Goliaths.

"I was a National Leaguer, so I've got to root for the National League club," he says.

"Was" a National Leaguer. Is it possible that seven years have elapsed since Phil Nastu threw his last professional pitch? Eight years since he last wore a major league uniform?

Have more than nine seasons passed since Phil Nastu, as a member of a San Francisco Giants' starting rotation that included Vida Blue, Bob Knepper and John Montefusco, pitched a complete-game, five-hit, 8–1 victory over the Houston Astros? Losing pitcher: J.R. Richard.

Phil Nastu. *1978 Cramer Sports Promotions.*

Nastu, Bridgeport born, bred and educated, has been a resident of the Park City for all of his thirty-three years, save for that unforgettable period when he had baseball addresses in San Francisco, Phoenix, Cedar Rapids, Iowa, and Midland, Texas. He still keeps a close watch on the game he played with a passion. "I watch it all the time."

His response to Kirk Gibson's dramatic ninth-inning home run, which put the Series' opening game in the Los Angeles win column, is a fanlike, "Oh, my goodness, that was great."

One could not blame him if he were bitter. When the Chicago Cubs decided he was expendable, in the spring of 1982, he had just celebrated his twenty-seventh birthday.

"The two springs with the Cubs were the best I ever had," he recalls, sitting in the living room of his comfortable home on Stratfield Place in the city's North End, the home he shares with his wife Joyce and their sons, Chris, twelve, and Lee, seven. "In 1982, I had a great Triple-A camp. I even called my wife and told her we were going to Des Moines. And then, on the last day of camp, they released me. What hurt was having pitched so well and getting cut, and then [their] doing it so late that I couldn't hook on with another club..."

Well, perhaps he harbors some ill feelings toward the Cubs. But his five years as a pro, with perhaps one-third of that time with San Francisco (1978–80), elicit more positive memories.

Think about it. Two years removed from the University of Bridgeport campus and he, a free agent signee, was a member of a team whose history included Mays, Ott, Hubbell and Marichal. Indeed, a Hall of Famer named Willie McCovey was a teammate. For much of the 1979 season, Nastu and Knepper were the left-handers in Manager Joe Altobelli's starting rotation.

"Nineteen seventy-nine was my most satisfying year because that's when they called me up in April, after Montefusco got hurt," he explained. "You go up there and get people out, and you get the respect of players. Inside yourself, you say, 'Hey, I belong here.'"

Nastu pitched highly creditable baseball for San Francisco that year. He started fifteen games for a club that finished twenty games under .500, winning three and losing four. However, there were occasions when he pitched well for five or six innings and then exited for a pinch-hitter.

The three wins were outstanding—the aforementioned decision over an Astro lineup that included such legitimate hitters as Bob Watson, Jose Cruz and Cesar Cedeno, and 2–1 and 3–2 verdicts over Cincinnati's Big Red Machine.

The memory brought a smile. "I was in the bullpen later in the year when we played the Reds again. [George] Foster and [Ken] Griffey told me, 'Nasty, thank God you're not starting. We don't want any part of you.'"

Perhaps J.R. Richard didn't either. Phil Nastu tagged the ill-fated Astro pitcher for an RBI single in their face-to-face confrontation.

Alas, the meteoric rise through the Giants' farm system to San Francisco was followed by an equally rapid descent. Within two years he was back home in Bridgeport.

What happened? A "left eye problem" the following year, which required rest and a series of tests at Stanford University before its origin was discovered, prevented him from pitching for two months. In essence, he lost a year. "My depth perception was really bad. I almost couldn't catch the throws from the catcher."

One night, he made the mistake of convincing the Phoenix manager, Rocky Bridges, that his vision was fine. Bridges handed him the ball. Ouch. He was plunked in the ribs by a line drive he never saw and collapsed in pain.

Today, Phil Nastu makes his starting assignments for Avco Lycoming, with which he is in his second year as an inventory analyst. It isn't Candlestick Park, but it's a decent living. Opportunities should exist for a man with a BA in industrial management.

For recreation, he played in "eighty to ninety" games this summer with two of the region's premier slow-pitch softball teams, Avco and Midas Touch Jewelers. Avco finished second in the National Industrial Tournament. Nastu, as the left center fielder, batted a composite .600 or thereabouts.

One suspects Phil derives as much pleasure from coaching his son in Little League. With the senior Nastu as coach (along with his brother-in-law Mark Marko), and Chris Nastu as an all-star infielder, the North End Pirates assembled a 21–3 record. "Chris," says his proud dad, "has good hand-eye coordination. He pitched well. I think he was eight and one."

So the man who was a two-sport athlete (basketball and baseball, in that order) at Bassick High School and UB, the man who for an instant lived his dream, can be found on Stratfield Place. He listens to Vin Scully describe a World Series. He works and he plays. "Our lives," he says, "are geared around our little guys."

Phil Nastu is home.

Bridgeport Light, October 26, 1988.

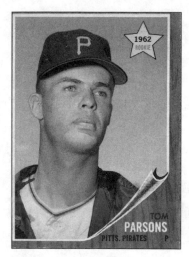

Tom Parsons. *1961 Topps.*

PARSONS SATISFIED WITH PERFORMANCE

San Francisco's Giants, the team with thunder in its bats, managed only scattered showers off the slants of Lakeville's Tom Parsons Saturday. The twenty-five-year-old Mets pitcher, making his first start of the season, pitched a creditable six innings against Mays, McCovey, Hart and company in the New Yorkers' 4–0 loss. True, Tommy surrendered nine hits, but all were singles—two of them cheapies.

"I was very satisfied with my pitching," Parsons said over the phone Saturday night. "My fast ball was moving and I broke off a few good curves."

With better support from second baseman Bobby Klaus, Tommy would have escaped with only one run scored instead of two.

With two down in the third inning and Jose Pagan on first, Klaus booted Hal Lanier's easy grounder, moving Pagan to second. Matty Alou followed with a sharp grounder directly at Klaus, and Bobby let it kick off his shins for a single. Pagan scored from second.

Parsons settled down and retired Mays—for the second straight time—to end the inning.

Tom also had good luck against Ed Bailey, the Giants catcher. Two of his three strikeouts came against Bailey. "I threw him low pitches all day," Tom recalled. "The first time I got behind him 3–0 with curves, and then I struck him out on three straight fast balls."

Parsons had two special reasons for pitching well yesterday. Their names are Donald Parsons, his father, and Toni, Tom's attractive wife.

His dad had never seen Tom pitch a big-league game before he made the hundred-mile trip from Lakeville to Shea Stadium Saturday. As for Toni, "she was as nervous as ever," Tom laughed.

Parsons now has given up but one earned run in eight innings, and that's not bad by any standards. Thus, Tom is moving toward a goal he's had almost since birth. Tom always wanted to be a pitcher.

Thomas Anthony Parsons came into this world on September 13, 1939, at Lakeville, Connecticut. Almost before Tom knew his right hand from his left, Donald Parsons began to mold him into a pitcher. Dad knew what he was talking about, too; he caught semipro ball with the Lakeville team for sixteen years.

Nobody knows pitchers like an old catcher.

"My dad and Ed Kirby, my high school coach, played the major roles in my early development," the soft-spoken right-hander explained.

Kirby, Housatonic Regional's well-regarded baseball coach, has been instrumental in five of his pitching pupils signing professional contracts. Besides Parsons, Steve Blass, who is now in his second year with Pittsburgh, the Lamb brothers, John and Art, and Jack Bristol are other Housatonic grads to play professionally. Parsons, Blass and the two Lambs are related.

"Steve and I keep in touch during the off-season," Tom said, "and our wives exchange letters when they get the chance."

Parsons, who stands six feet, seven inches tall, was a gangling six-five when Kirby had him at Regional, but right away the coach saw tremendous potential. By his senior year, opposing batters had trouble getting even the proverbial loud foul.

That's no exaggeration. Parson pitched *four* no-hitters as a senior, and most of his other victories were one- and two-hitters. Once he fanned twenty-one batters in a seven-inning game.

Major league scouts, who rarely miss a prospect, came up to Falls Village by the carload for most of Tom's late-season games. The day he struck out twenty-one, such knowledgeable baseball men as Harry Hesse of the Yankees and the Cubs' Lennie Merullo were in the stands.

They were wasting their time, though. Pittsburgh had the inside track from the beginning because Kirby worked for the Pirates organization as a sub scout, or "bird dog."

So, following graduation in 1957, Tom signed a Pittsburgh contract and reported to Salem of the Appalachian League. Starting fast, Tom's blazing fastball fanned 135 batters in ninety-six innings as he captured eight of twelve decisions. Moving up the ladder a rung at a time, Tom pitched in places like Grand Forks, Idaho Falls, Salt Lake City and finally, in 1961, Columbus, the Bucs' number one farm.

At this point, however, Tom's career turned into a nightmare of injuries and frustrations. As Tom tells it: "I was pitching for Columbus one night early in the 1961 season when I hurt my arm. After pitching four and a third innings, my arm began to tighten up. I retired the next batter, but that was it. I couldn't get the third out."

Disillusioned, Tom sat out the next nine weeks. He didn't know if he'd ever be able to pitch with his former effectiveness. "I couldn't throw a curve at all." Recovery was a slow process. It wasn't until late 1962 that Parsons could throw a curveball again.

The Pirates, to their credit, didn't give up on him. From 1958 through '64, Tom went to spring training with the parent club. Sometimes he impressed, sometimes he didn't, but Pittsburgh always brought him back.

The Bucs thought enough of his 1963 pitching at Columbus to promote him at the tail end of the season, and "that's when I hurt my shoulder. I started against the Braves at Milwaukee and got hit pretty hard," Tom says matter-of-factly. "My shoulder was hurting when I left after the fourth."

So it did. He had tendonitis.

Parsons entered the U.S. Marines in September of that year, and he credits rope-pulling exercises with aiding his recovery. "The eight years I spent in the minors didn't get me down," Tom confesses, "but those injuries sure kept me awake nights."

The year 1964 was a happy one for Parsons on two counts: 1) he got married and 2) the Mets purchased his contract.

Training that spring with the Bucs at Fort Myers, Florida, Tom wooed and won pretty Antoinette Blake. Toni was raised in Canton, Ohio, but, fortunately for Tom, the Blake family later migrated to Florida. Tom and Toni were married on June 4. They'll add a little right-hander to the staff some time in late September.

The Mets obtained his contract—he was one of their many conditional purchases—after hearing fine reports on his pitching at Oklahoma City, a Houston farm. Tom was still Pittsburgh property, though, having been on loan.

"Pittsburgh treated me fairly," Tom says in retrospect, "but I was happy to be with the Mets. I felt I was really wanted."

Desperate for pitching, the Mets' Casey Stengel threw the elongated righty against the Giants on September 15, just a day after he reported, and Tom responded with two innings of shutout relief. A 1–0, six-hit loss to Houston's Bob Bruce and a one-run, five-inning relief win against the Cards—on the next-to-last day of the season—convinced the Mets they hadn't made a mistake.

After yesterday's game, the Giants are probably in agreement.

Waterbury Republican, April 18, 1965.

THE TWISTS AND TURNS OF
PRETZELS PEZZULLO

Pretzels Pezzullo. Unless you dabble in baseball minutiae or have joined the growing ranks of senior citizens, this colorful name probably draws a blank. John "Pretzels" Pezzullo. In the Depression years of the 1930s, few pitchers were faster than this left-hander with the unforgettable nickname.

So explosive was his fastball that it enabled him to spend one season and a portion of another with the Philadelphia Phillies in an era when Mel Ott, Joe Medwick and Wally Berger were the National League's reigning sluggers.

Born and raised in Bridgeport, Pezzullo celebrated his seventy-eighth birthday on December 10, but his health has deteriorated and he prefers to keep to himself. You will find him in Dallas, with his wife Betty (née Tolcyk), where they have resided for the past forty years.

On most occasions, he is reluctant to answer the telephone. When cancer was detected many years ago, surgeons were forced to remove a portion of his jaw, and his speech is not easily understood. His memories of those baseball summers of long ago are left unshared with outsiders.

Well, some people remember. They recall the pitcher who blew away hitters on hot afternoons at Seaside Park; the man who pitched for the White Eagles, Holy Rosary, McKesson & Robbins and other leading local teams before the professionals took notice. They remember Pretzels Pezzullo.

"A man whose uncle was a part owner with Indianapolis of the American Association, which was affiliated with the New York Giants, got him a tryout in the Polo Grounds," says Jim Pezzullo, John's brother and, at eighty-one, the oldest of four Pezzullo siblings.

"He had to go down there seven or eight days. No expenses. One time, the catcher, Gus Mancuso, called him over and said, 'Let me

Pretzels Pezzullo. *Courtesy of the Pezzullo family.*

see your hard one.' My brother could throw pretty fast. I think Mancuso was impressed."

Jim Pezzullo doesn't remember the year; he isn't too accurate on dates. But it must have been 1931 or '32 when the Depression had Bridgeport firmly in its grasp. Jobs were scarce and honest dollars were hard to come by.

Jim, who lives with Kay, his wife of fifty-four years, on Huntington Road in the city's Upper East Side, hasn't seen Pretzels in "at least fifteen years." And it's been awhile since they communicated by phone. But one can detect a sense of pride when he talks of his brother's pitching accomplishments.

"John was a fast-ball pitcher, but wild. Before he went with the pros, he pitched for the McKesson & Robbins team in the Industrial League. They hired the best ballplayers. They would pick him up at ten o'clock on a Sunday morning and play all over the state."

Thanks to his tryout in the old Polo Grounds in New York City, Pretzels soon made the quantum leap into pro ball and the Giants' farm system. As the 1930s progressed, he wore flannel uniforms for several cities; Hazelton, Atlanta, Richmond, Savannah, Toronto and, for all of 1935 and a slice of the 1936 season, Philadelphia. Wherever he pitched, Pezzullo fastballs frightened hitters.

"He was a helluva fast ball pitcher, no control. No curve. He was real, real fast. When you were up there, you were dying to get away from the plate," remembers eighty-year-old Lenny Benedetto, once an amateur first baseman of considerable skill and Pretzels's close friend. "He lived on Orchard Street. I lived where [Father] Panik Village is now. It was called Hell's Kitchen. We used to warm up there and he was always hitting the wall of the building. I gave him his nickname because of his crazy windup. We played together with Holy Rosary. I coached the team. I'd say he [his fastball] was in the nineties, ninety-five. He'd strike out fourteen, fifteen, sixteen in a game. All smoke."

That "smoke" brought Pezzullo into the National League in 1935, following a multi-player trade that sent him from the Giants to the Phillies in exchange for shortstop Dick Bartell. The Phils, managed by the old catcher, Jimmy Wilson, were a sad-sack seventh-place club that season, losing 89 of 153 games.

There were a few stars in the lineup, notably the first baseman, Dolph Camilli, who was to reach the heights with the Brooklyn Dodgers, and outfielders Johnny Moore (from Waterbury) and Ethan Allen.

Wilson employed Pezzullo as a relief pitcher, but seven starting assignments were included among his forty-two appearances. He won three games and lost five. Against Pretzels's fastballs, twenty-four National League hitters went down on strikes.

Benedetto said, "If he won three games, they must have been against Pittsburgh. The Waner brothers [Hall of Famers Paul and Lloyd] couldn't touch him."

Unable to find a modicum of control, Pezzullo was farmed out to Richmond of the Piedmont League in 1936. He never got back to the top, although he pitched with skill on minor league baseball's higher rungs as the 1930s drew to a close.

A superlative 1938 season with Savannah of the Sally League—he led the league with twenty-six victories, 288 innings and 218 strikeouts, including seventeen in a single game—earned Pretzels a spring trial with the Boston Braves in 1939. It didn't pan out.

If Pretzels Pezzullo has been out of sight since the late 1940s, when he relocated to Dallas with his employer, Chance Vought, he is not out of the minds of those who saw him play. Recalls Fred Vercini, seventy-nine, the retired sports editor of the *Bridgeport Post*: "He threw the ball like hell. He was a helluva prospect."

John Takacs, seventy-nine, a former fireman who was a top-flight amateur pitcher in the 1930s, describes Pezzullo as "a great left-handed pitcher with the McKesson team. He was very fast."

If Pretzels Pezzullo is unable to communicate by telephone, it's safe to assume he would be receptive to a card or a letter during the holiday season. Write him at 3127 West Ledbetter Drive, Dallas, TX 75233.

Bridgeport Light, December 27, 1989.

PIERSALL AT DUSK:
STILL CANDID, COMBATIVE, COLORFUL

WESTPORT—An eight-year-old boy extends his hand with reluctance. The elderly man sitting on the other side of the table envelopes the boy's hand in his and offers a warm smile.

"Shake hands like a man," Jim Piersall tells the boy as he pumps his hand.

The boy manages a shy smile, accepts an autographed photo from one of the game's greatest defensive center fielders and ambles off.

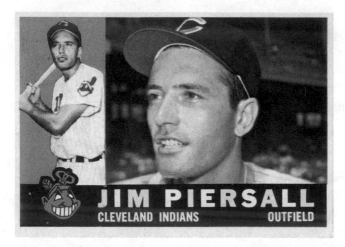

Jimmy Piersall.
1960 Topps.

This was a frequent scene at Legends of the Game, a sports memorabilia shop in the Compo Shopping Center, on a Sunday afternoon in early September. Boys, men of varying ages and a few women queued up to meet the outfielder who transformed defensive play into an art form.

"I used to deliver papers to your house," said a man named Tom Griffin, who made the trek from Waterbury to Westport to see Piersall.

The old outfielder smiles at their connection. "Well, that must have been a long time ago," he tells Griffin before signing.

If you followed baseball during the 1950s and '60s, you knew Jimmy Piersall. From his clashes with fans, umpires and opposing players to his backward trot around the bases to mark his one hundredth career home run, Piersall brought a rainbow of color and a bit of zaniness to the field. Across seventeen seasons, he hit .272 and 104 homers with five clubs and was selected to two all-star teams.

On and off the field, Piersall often couldn't control himself, which nearly led to his early exit from baseball and, in 1952, his commitment to a mental hospital. His comeback the following season provided the impetus for his autobiography, *Fear Strikes Out*, written with the late Al Hirshberg. A biopic with the same title followed in 1957, starring the miscast Anthony Perkins as Piersall and the talented Karl Malden as his overbearing father.

Piersall has disowned the film. "I didn't climb *no* screen," he wailed. "My father wasn't as tough as they made him out to be."

For this appearance in Westport, a speaking engagement at the Hartford World Series Club the following night and a couple of other stops, Piersall had flown from Chicago to Boston. He and his third wife, Jan, share a home in suburban Wheaton, Illinois, and winter in Scottsdale, Arizona.

On this trip, there would be no visit to his native Waterbury, a once-flourishing city of 107,000 in the Naugatuck Valley. "I was there five years ago. It's really a crime what they've done to that city. It makes me sick," Piersall said. "I said to the mayor, 'If I give you a thousand bucks, will you fix it up?' He told me, 'Don't bother. It'll only get dirty again.'"

James Anthony Piersall, born November 14, 1929, rose from the Waterbury sandlots to wear the uniform of the team he rooted for as a youngster—the Boston Red Sox. He was just twenty years old when he joined the club in September 1950. This was the powerful team of Ted Williams, Bobby Doerr, Dom DiMaggio, Vern Stephens, Johnny Pesky, Walt Dropo, Billy Goodman, Mel Parnell and Ellis Kinder.

"All the Italians in Waterbury were Yankee fans. I hated the Yankees from the time I left my mother's womb," he recalled. "I loved the Red Sox…Jimmie Foxx, Bobby Doerr, Ted Williams…How many kids grow up rooting for a team and then get to play for them? Dom DiMaggio was one of the really great players, one of the five best leadoff hitters of all time. It's a crime he isn't in the Hall of Fame."

Piersall's earliest acclaim came in another sport—basketball. An energetic forward with quick moves, he led Leavenworth High School (the forerunner of John F. Kennedy High) to the 1947 New England scholastic championship, scoring twenty-nine points in the title game against Durfee (Massachusetts) High in Boston Garden.

So the story goes, a Red Sox scout was in the Garden that evening. "Can he play baseball?" the scout asked somebody in the Waterbury contingent. "He's even better in baseball," the scout was told.

Piersall signed a free-agent contract with the Red Sox after high school and began the climb up the minor league ladder. In 1948, he played for Boston's Class-A affiliate at Scranton, Pennsylvania, where he met Mary Teevan. They were married in October 1949, following his first season at Triple-A Louisville. By the time he was thirty-one years old, the Piersalls were the parents of nine children.

He claims to have no recollections of the 1952 season with Boston, when he displayed signs of the mental illness that had plagued his mother. He fought with the Yankees' combative second baseman, Billy Martin, and even a teammate, Mickey McDermott, and antagonized fans and umpires.

His erratic behavior led to his being demoted to Double-A Birmingham. Three weeks later, Piersall entered a Massachusetts state hospital for psychiatric treatment. He was diagnosed with manic depression, treated with electroshock therapy and released after six weeks.

"Mr. [Tom] Yawkey [the Red Sox's owner] sent me to Florida for the whole winter and picked up the tab," Piersall recalled.

Rejoining the Red Sox in 1953, a recovered Piersall became an integral part of the club for six seasons, at first playing right field and then moving to center, where he was flanked by the great Williams in left and Jackie Jensen in right. "A complete player," he says of Jensen.

In the opener of a 1953 doubleheader against the St. Louis Browns, Piersall went six for six at bat, tying the American League record for hits in a nine-inning game. He batted .272 that year.

In 1954, he was selected to the All-Star Game for the first time. His second all-star selection, in 1956, came during his finest all-around season when he hit .293, drove in eighty-seven runs, scored ninety-one runs and collected fourteen home runs and a league-leading forty doubles.

Piersall was voted the Red Sox's Most Valuable Player that season, no mean feat considering that Williams (the consummate hitter and a two-time American League Most Valuable Player) and Jensen (who would win the 1958 American League MVP award) were among his teammates.

In the outfield, Piersall become renowned for his acrobatic, leaping catches. Twice, in 1958 and in 1961 with the Cleveland Indians, he won the Gold Glove Award. For statistical proof, the Piersall career fielding percentage, .990, ranks among the highest of all time.

Casey Stengel, who managed championship Yankee teams from 1949 through 1960, once called Piersall the most natural defensive outfielder he'd ever seen. As player and manager, Stengel was associated with the game for nearly sixty years—he managed DiMaggio and Mantle, he saw Mays and Snider—so that statement carries considerable weight.

Stengel was Piersall's manager with the Mets in 1963, when, on June 23 in the Polo Grounds, he hit the one hundredth home run of his career against the Philadelphia Phillies. He celebrated the occasion by circling the bases backward—albeit in the right direction.

How would Jim Piersall compare today's players with those from his era?

"We were better trained...how to think the game, how to execute," he responded. "Today, a lot of times you see a player get picked off with the score 7–0."

He gets up from his chair and assumes the stance of an outfielder. "The center fielder has to know how to move the other outfielders. Never stand directly behind second base. Play to the right side or the left side so you can see the plate."

After his playing career ended in 1967 with the Los Angeles Angels, Piersall remained in the game in several capacities. He was director of group sales for the Oakland Athletics under Charley Finley. In 1975, he was hired by his former sparring partner, Martin, to tutor the Texas Rangers outfielders.

Two years later, the Chicago White Sox made the always-candid Piersall a broadcaster and teamed him with Harry Caray. In 1983, he was dismissed for being too critical of White Sox management. A second book, *The Truth Hurts*, published in 1985, discusses his ouster and also addresses his struggles with bipolar disorder.

Then, as a roving minor league outfield instructor with the Chicago Cubs, Piersall shared his expertise with prospects and would-be prospects from 1986 to 1999. They couldn't have asked for a more knowledgeable— or entertaining—instructor.

Greenwich Citizen, September 21, 2007.

OLD GREENWICH'S GIFT TO MAJORS

In the summer of 1942, September 19 fell on a Saturday, and the news on most fronts was disturbing. Russian troops were fighting for the very life of Stalingrad against the Nazis, who were ordered to take the city at any cost. In the Pacific, U.S. Marines were holding the airfield on Guadalcanal in the Solomon Islands, despite repeated attacks by the Japanese.

On another ominous note, Pope Pius XII granted an audience to President Roosevelt's personal representative to the Vatican; they reportedly discussed anti-Semitic developments in Vichy France.

Much closer to home, September 19 was also the day that a twenty-six-year-old native of Old Greenwich appeared in a major league game for the first time. The site was Braves Field, Boston. Pinch-hitting for Boston shortstop Whitey Weitelmann in the eighth inning, Mike Sandlock lined a single up the middle against New York Giants reliever Fiddler Bill McGee. Sandlock would eventually score on Clyde Kluttz's two-run triple.

The Giants won the game, though, thanks to a bases-filled home run by Mel Ott. Score: Giants seven, Braves six.

"That was the best drinking club I ever ran into," Sandlock said of the 1942 Braves. He didn't name names, but Casey Stengel—still several years removed from being anointed a managerial genius with the Yankees—was the club's manager, and Paul Waner played left field. Both men were on friendly terms with the bottle. Both would be elected to the game's Hall of Fame.

"Casey Stengel didn't help me at all," Sandlock said. "But I got tips from Al Lopez—remember him? He gave me instructions, showed me how to get rid of the ball quick."

For sixteen summers, many of them glorious, Michael Joseph Sandlock earned his livelihood at ballparks throughout the contiguous United States. "Have glove and bat, will travel." He was a switch-hitting catcher—sometimes an infielder—talented enough to play for three National League teams, the Braves, Brooklyn Dodgers and Pittsburgh Pirates, over five seasons. He also played at the game's next highest level, Triple A, for eight years, at San Diego, Hollywood, Montreal and St. Paul. All of those municipalities are part of today's major league landscape.

Today, you will find Mike Sandlock at 20 Rockland Place in Old Greenwich, the same street on which he grew to manhood during the Depression. He is eighty-seven years old, but sturdily built, about six feet tall and 190 pounds, still capable of driving a golf ball with authority at Innis Arden.

"I'm a sixteen handicap now. No more seventies for me," he said.

The front porch at 20 Rockland is crammed with memorabilia from Sandlock's playing career. Scrapbooks, carefully assembled by his late wife, Victoria. Dozens of photographs. Programs. Plastic-enclosed letters from Dodger President Branch Rickey and Fred Haney, who was his manager in Hollywood and Pittsburgh. Baseball cards, including Mike's own 1953 and '54 Topps cards.

Mike Sandlock. *1953 Topps*.

He pulls out a photograph of Joe DiMaggio swinging a bat, shot at an exhibition game on the West Coast in the fall of 1951. "That was Joe's last (albeit unofficial) at-bat," Sandlock says. The catcher behind the plate is—yes—Mike Sandlock.

Sandlock wasn't a star at the major league level, but he was a teammate of many who were. He caught Hall of Famer Warren Spahn with Evansville of the Three-I League. He was with Spahn, Waner, Stengel and a fourth Hall of Famer, Ernie Lombardi, on the 1942 Braves.

He struck up a friendship with Hall of Fame catcher Roy Campanella in 1947, when both wore the uniform of the Montreal Royals of the International League. "The nicest little chap, very friendly," he says of Campy. "We went to Cuba for spring training."

The following summer, Sandlock's Montreal teammates included Hall of Fame center fielder Duke Snider, pitcher Don Newcombe and a lanky first baseman named Kevin Connors. "Moody," he says of Snider, the slugging outfielder who led Brooklyn to five pennants in an eight-year span. "Newcombe, he threw hard and heavy. My hand used to puff up after catching him."

Connors, an elongated six-foot-five, reached the majors with Brooklyn and the Chicago Cubs, but became better known in later years as the actor Chuck Connors, star of *The Rifleman* on television and a featured player in films.

When Sandlock reached Pittsburgh in the spring of 1953, a seven-time home run king, Ralph Kiner, still wore Pirate flannels. Joe Garagiola, a catcher who would become a nationally known broadcaster and raconteur, was there. And so was another Greenwich native, infielder Pete Castiglione. Before the season had run its course, all three were traded. "He had a short fuse," Sandlock said of Castiglione.

The son of Polish immigrants, Sandlock grew up in Old Greenwich when it was known as Sound Beach. He gestures to the street beyond the porch. "This used to be a dirt road. There used to be cattle next door, haystacks over there."

His formal education was limited to Sound Beach School and a couple of years at Wright Tech in Stamford. That was it. Then he went off to work at the Electrolux plant and played industrial league ball with the Cos Cob Fire Department and other teams. In 1937, he impressed Boston Bees scouts in a tryout, and they signed him to a professional contract.

"I was making $200 a month at Electrolux. My first year I got $75 a month to play at Huntington, West Virginia, in the Mountain State

League," he said. "My father used to say working in a factory is like going to jail. They open the gate in the morning and they don't let you out until it's time to quit."

Sandlock's rise through the Bees/Braves' farm system was rapid. He hit a sound .277 at Huntington in 1938, and an even .300 with Bradford, Pennsylvania, the following year, when he was voted the Pony League's all-star catcher. He was relegated to backup duty with Hartford of the Eastern League in 1940, but quickly rebounded with successive .320 and .307 seasons with Evansville, earning that late-season promotion to Boston in September 1942.

He appeared in two games at short, finishing with one hit in one at-bat, which translates into a 1.000 batting average.

With World War II in full flame, Sandlock sat out the 1943 season and worked in an Evansville plant that built fighter planes. He rejoined the Braves for thirty games in 1944 before his contract was sold to the Dodgers. That set the stage for his finest National League season.

With a third-place Brooklyn team in 1945, Sandlock appeared in eighty games—primarily behind the plate—and batted a fine .282. Leo "the Lip" Durocher was the manager. "He really wanted to win. To me, he was a good manager," Sandlock recalled. "His wife, [actress] Laraine Day, was a very nice person. She'd play cards with you."

Both of Sandlock's National League home runs came that year, both, curiously, off the same pitcher, Harry Feldman of the Giants. "My first home run was in the Polo Grounds. The second hit the clock on the scoreboard at Ebbets Field."

The season ended, but the baseball didn't. In December, Sandlock was among a group of major league players that made a USO-sponsored tour across the country, facing U.S. service teams at military bases stateside and then in Hawaii (still a territory) and the Philippines. They returned home exhausted but happy at the end of January.

"Some of the flights were pretty scary," he remembered. "We played Stan Musial's [navy] team in Hawaii and we ran into [Dodger pitcher] Kirby Higbe in the Philippines." Frank McCormick, Whitey Kurowski, Ralph Branca and Red Barrett were among Sandlock's notable teammates.

With the war over and a flock of stars returning from the service, major league rosters were overstocked in the spring of 1946. Sandlock spent the first portion of the year with Brooklyn, then was reassigned to St. Paul of the American Association. He was destined to spend the remainder of his career at the Triple-A or Open level, save for the season in Pittsburgh.

Sandlock has no complaints, though. "The best time I had (in the game) was out on the coast," he said. "Some of the teams in the Pacific Coast League (PCL) were better than some of the National League teams at the time."

No question. Many stars on the way down—Joe Gordon, Luke Easter, Max West, Walt Judnich—were quite content to finish up in the PCL. Johnny Lindell, the former Yankee outfielder, spent a couple of years perfecting a knuckleball with Hollywood and, as a pitcher, accompanied Sandlock to Pittsburgh.

God's sunlight always seemed to shine in Hollywood. And the money was good, too. "I was making ten grand a year out there," Sandlock said.

For four seasons (1949–52), he was Hollywood's regular catcher, a period in which the Stars (as they were appropriately known) won two PCL championships. Show business personalities of the day—George Burns and Gracie Allen, Jack Benny, Phil Silvers, Mickey Rooney, Pat O'Brien, Chill Wills—populated the stands at Gilmore Field, to see and to be seen. The man who portrayed Fred Mertz on *I Love Lucy*, William Frawley, was a co-owner of the club.

Life was decidedly less glamorous in Pittsburgh. The 1953 Pirates, a mix of graybeards and kids, finished last in the eight-team National League. Sandlock shared the catching with Garagiola and Vic Janowicz, who had been a Heisman Trophy–winning running back at Ohio State, and batted .231 across sixty-four games.

For Sandlock, the year's highlight was "Mike Sandlock Day" at the Polo Grounds in New York. A group of fans from Greenwich and Stamford presented him with a new Dodge and other gifts on the field as his wife and two children, Mike Jr. and Mary Ellen, beamed. (A third child, Damon, was born several years later.)

Sold to the Phillies in the off-season, Sandlock appeared to have won a roster spot on the 1954 club until he suffered a severe knee injury about a week prior to the season. "We were playing an exhibition game in Schenectady, and this young kid came barreling into to me at the plate. He was out from here to Broadway, but…"

A major "but." The next uniform he wore was that of the Phillies' Triple-A club in San Diego, where the thirty-eight-year-old Sandlock helped the Padres win the PCL title in a one-game playoff with—yes— Hollywood. End of story. Or almost.

On April 30, 1998, Mike Sandlock was inducted into the Brooklyn Dodgers Hall of Fame, permanently reuniting him with Newcombe, Branca, Tommy Brown and several other former teammates.

Just five weeks ago, the old catcher had a chance encounter with a former batterymate. "Newcombe gave me the biggest hug," said Sandlock, smiling, "when I saw him at a card show on Long Island."

Greenwich Citizen, July 18, 2003.

SHEA: MEMORIES OF A MEMORABLE YANKEE YEAR

Joe DiMaggio is sitting in the passenger seat of a new Hudson, a stack of mail placed neatly on his lap. He opens an envelope. A check appears. He opens another envelope. Another check.

"By the time we got to the ballpark, he had $12,000 dollars in endorsements," remembered Frank "Spec" Shea, in whose automobile the Yankees Clipper was riding.

Shea provided frequent livery service for DiMaggio during their years together with the New York Yankees. Likable and loquacious, the pitcher enjoyed a special friendship with what many experts believe is baseball's greatest living player, a man who could be aloof.

"He used to buy me breakfast every day at the hotel. He'd never let me pay," Shea said. "I never treated DiMaggio like God. He was an everyday guy as far as I was concerned."

As another World Series begins, Frank Joseph Shea, at seventy-three, may be found in the hills of his native Naugatuck. Frank and Genevieve Shea have lived in the same house for forty-four years, the comfortable home on Johnson Street he had built for them as newlyweds and where they raised their three children.

He is synonymous with the factory town that became known for its production of rubber. "The Naugatuck Nugget" he was called in his heyday.

Spec Shea was an important pitcher for the postwar Yankees, a major contributor to the 1947 World Series and a bit player on two other pennant-winning clubs, in 1949 and 1951. DiMaggio was the undisputed star of these teams, a center fielder without peer and a hitter second only to Ted Williams in the American League. Shea was part of an uncommonly deep supporting cast—outfielder Tommy Henrich, known

Frank "Spec" Shea. *1950 Bowman.*

as Old Reliable; the consummate shortstop Phil Rizzuto; Hall of Fame catcher Yogi Berra; and pitchers Allie Reynolds, Vic Raschi, Eddie Lopat and Joe Page.

No first-year pitcher of postwar vintage has been able to duplicate Shea's 1947 rookie season. He was twenty-six years old, a veteran of three years of service with the Army Air Corps during World War II, when he arrived at Yankee Stadium. Older and more mature than the typical rookie, he was a hit with the team he had adored as a youngster.

"I grew up as a Yankee fan," he said. "My father took me down to the stadium when I was a kid, and this was when you could go on the field after the game. I used to run out to the mound and pretend I was pitching. 'Someday,' I'd say, 'I'm going to pitch here.'"

And he did. Before his first American League season had run its course, Shea assembled a fourteen-win, five-loss record, topping the league in winning percentage (.737) and fewest hits allowed in nine innings (6.40). He also ranked eighth in earned run average, with 3.07 (behind such luminaries as Bob Feller and Hal Newhouser, but ahead of teammate Allie Reynolds).

Thanks in part to Shea's mastery of the second-place Detroit Tigers, the Yankees, under first-year manager Bucky Harris, won the pennant by twelve games. Three times that summer he prevailed in duels with Tiger ace Newhouser, twice winning by a shutout.

Naugatuck residents, thrilled by his early successes, turned out en masse to honor their native son at Yankee Stadium on June 22. A day for a rookie is unusual, but it attested to the high esteem in which he was held by fellow Nutmeggers.

The crowd of 53,765 included thousands from Connecticut who had purchased tickets weeks in advance in the hope of seeing Shea pitch. (He didn't.) The Borough of Naugatuck's warden, Harry L. Carter, presented Shea with a 1947 maroon Hudson, complete with the Connecticut license plate SPEC.

On July 8, the Naugatuck Nugget became the first rookie pitcher to receive credit for a victory in the All-Star Game, pitching the middle three innings of the American League's 2–1 decision over the National League at Wrigley Field in Chicago. He allowed the Nationals' lone run: Johnny Mize's home run in the fourth inning.

If Shea found himself upstaged in the World Series, it was understandable. For drama and deeds of derring-do, the 1947 Series ranks among the most memorable; this was the fall classic of Bill Bevens's flirtation with a no-hitter—which ended in defeat, courtesy of a two-out, game-winning double by Brooklyn's Cookie Lavagetto in the bottom of the ninth inning—and Al Gionfriddo's catch of DiMaggio's 415-foot wallop to left center field. It was also notable for the first appearance in a World Series of a black player, Jackie Robinson of Brooklyn.

But the stocky right-hander proved more than a match for the upstart Dodgers by winning two games. He captured the opener by a 5–3 score, allowing just one run and two hits in five innings before a record Series crowd of 73,365 at Yankee Stadium. The day after Bevens came up short in his no-hit attempt, Shea reestablished the Yankees' superiority by stopping the Dodgers, 2–1, on a four-hitter in game five at Ebbets Field. In a fitting coda, he fired a third strike past the previous day's hero, Lavagetto, for the final out. The Yankees, as was their custom, won the Series in seven games.

Shea recalled, "Everything I touched turned to gold that year. Getting credit for the win in the All-Star Game. Two victories in the World Series. How fortunate I was. It was a year you dream about. The only thing I feel bad about was I hurt my arm that year. I had no problem winning in the big leagues."

Never again did Spec Shea experience a year of that magnitude. The arm maladies that kept him on the sidelines for several weeks late in the 1947 season necessitated his return to the minor leagues in 1949. With an established Big Three corps of starters in Raschi, Reynolds and Lopat and Whitey Ford waiting in the wings, he was deemed expendable.

On May 3, 1952, Shea accompanied outfielder Jackie Jensen to the Washington Senators in a six-player trade that brought outfielder Irv Noren to New York. Was he disappointed? Not in the least.

"Hey, that trade reunited me with Bucky Harris, and he gave me a chance to pitch," Shea said. "The owner, Clark Griffith, who was a grand guy, told me I wouldn't be making any World Series money here and he handed me a $2,500 check when I arrived to make me feel welcome."

With fifth-place Senator teams, Shea proved a solid number two starter behind Bob Porterfield, turning in records of 11–7 in 1952 and 12–7 in 1953. He even contributed to the Yankees' pennant in the latter year by defeating runner-up Cleveland four times without a loss.

When his playing career ended after the 1955 season, Shea returned to the town of his birth with a creditable 56–46 record. He spent recent years as Naugatuck's superintendent of parks and recreation. In retirement, he remains visible by attending sports banquets and participating in charity golf tournaments with former big leaguers like Willard Marshall, Sal Yvars, Ralph Branca and Gene Hermanski. There are six grandchildren upon whom he lavishes time and love.

Shea, who was considered a tenacious negotiator during his playing days, insists he harbors no ill feelings toward today's players and their high salaries. "If I was playing ball today and I had a good year, I'd go in and fight for as much as I could get," said Shea, who was able to wring a $10,000 contract from the Yankees in 1947—when the major league minimum was half that amount. His peak salary was $28,000.

"But I've got to admit things have gotten out of hand. What does [Barry] Bonds make a game, $44,000? The only ones to blame are the owners. Television is going to put its foot down, and then we'll see what happens."

New York Times, October 17, 1993

SHELDON WOULD RATHER START

NEW YORK—Roland Frank Sheldon, the Connecticut Yankee in King John's court, has the lament of any reliever. "I'd rather start," he declares.

"Sheldon won't be a starter, at least right now," says his manager, Johnny Keane.

Keane seems to have the right idea, because reliever Sheldon has been highly effective this season. And if Yankee starters continue to get rocked, Rollie's going to come in handy.

"Keane is using me as a long reliever (with Billy Stafford)," Sheldon was saying the other day at Yankee Stadium. "And until the schedule gets heavier, he won't need more than four starters." He sighed.

They would be Mel Stottlemyre, Jim Bouton, Al Downing and Whitey Ford. But if Ford isn't healthy…

Maybe Rollie Sheldon doesn't particularly love his current task, but it's safe to say the batters don't have a crush on the Putnam, Connecticut native either.

The tall, slim right-hander has appeared twice in relief, and has a 0.00 earned run average to show for it. He's pitched five and a third innings, allowed no runs, only four hits—all singles—and walked none. What's more, Rollie's regained his fastball, as seven strikeouts will attest.

Sheldon couldn't have picked a more opportune time to show Keane and CBS that he's a capable big leaguer. With the trading deadline approaching, the Yankees figure to deal off one or two pitchers. Hal Reniff seems certain to go, and Stafford's status is shaky.

After a horrendous spring, Sheldon was in the same boat—the one bound for Toledo, the Bombers' new International League farm club—until he went out and blanked Kansas City and Minnesota in relief.

Which hitters have been toughest for Rollie? "All of them," he laughed. "Seriously, I found Jim Landis the toughest until I learned how to pitch him. Harmon Killebrew also hits me pretty good," he continued. "During that hot streak of his last summer, I threw him what I thought was a perfect pitch, and he hit it out of here."

Rollie Sheldon. *1962 Topps.*

Killebrew, the village smithy of the American League, kept up his one-man assault on Sheldon Thursday. Rollie replaced Downing in the second inning with two on, two out and three runs in and put out the fire, proceeding to blank the homer-happy Minnesotans over the next three innings on three singles. Killer had two of them.

Though twenty-eight years old, Sheldon looks as if he just stepped off the University of Connecticut campus—which, indeed, he did do some five years ago when Yankee scout Harry Hesse signed him. "I attended classes during the off-season from 1960 until February of this year when I finally received my degree," he explained.

Rollie is a rarity: he didn't pitch professionally until he was twenty-three. Today, most youngsters sign contracts right after high school, and a month or so later enter pro ball. Not Sheldon. He spent two and a half years overseas in the service and attended two colleges before signing a Yank contract.

Rollie tried Texas A&M as a freshman (in 1958) before transferring to UConn. Oddly, he gained more fame as a basketball player with the Huskies, sparking the 1959–60 quintet to an NCAA berth. He averaged something like 13.5 points a game and was a powerful rebounder.

"I played a few games with the East Hartford Explorers last winter," said the six-foot-four pitcher, "just to keep in shape."

That's traveling in fast company. The Explorers, boasting such former college stars as Paul (Topsy) DelGobbo and Ed Slomcenski, won the championship of the New England Basketball Association this past season.

Sheldon must enjoy competing in fast company. Signed to a Bomber contract in June 1960, Rollie compiled a 15–1 record with the Yankees' Class D Auburn, New York farm club that year, then went straight up to the varsity in 1961.

Sheldon won the James P. Dawson Memorial Award that spring as the outstanding Yankee rookie and, living up to his potential, won eleven games and dropped only five for a splendid first season. He alternated between starting and relieving.

As quickly as he climbed, that's how fast he fell back the next two seasons. He slipped to 7–8 (with a 5.49 ERA) in '62. The following year he slipped all the way to Richmond and then the to the Bombers' Illinois farm. The country air wasn't beneficial at first as he captured only five of fourteen decisions in '63.

The year 1964 found the crew-cut hurler back in form. At Richmond, he posted a 1.85 ERA and won four and lost two, prompting his recall on June 12. Rollie then became a key man in the Bombers' late-season pennant push, winning five of seven decisions. His control was remarkable as he walked only eighteen in 102 innings.

Wine and Warren Spahn improve with age. So does Roland Frank Sheldon, it seems.

Waterbury Republican, April 25, 1965.

SHOPAY CATCHING ON

NEW YORK—As the smallest catcher this side of the Pony League, five-foot-nine, 160-pound Tom Shopay is taking a lot of kidding these days.

"You've got to be a low-ball catcher," needled Joe Garagiola, the catcher-turned-broadcaster, during the Orioles' batting practice at Shea Stadium Saturday.

"You're a sinker ball catcher," chimed in Tony Kubek, the shortstop-turned-broadcaster.

"Hey, Tommy," shouted Thurman Munson, the Yankee catcher who stands a compact five-foot-ten himself, "which of us is taller?"

Tom Shopay merely smiles at the one-liners being tossed in his direction. Occasionally he even pokes fun at himself. "I'm the only catcher who can give the signs standing up," he has said, a quote that appears in this week's issue of *Sports Illustrated*.

The Bristol-born Shopay, no dumbbell he, reasons that it's better to be the smallest catcher in the major leagues than the number two hitter in the International League, a ranking he held last year when he batted .313 for Rochester.

"After this year, I'll only need thirty-seven days to qualify for the Major League pension," he said. "I'd like to hang on for another year or two."

Heretofore strictly an outfielder, Shopay has been the Orioles' third-string catcher since mid-June, or just after Andy Etchebarren was sold to the California Angels. Although never having caught in ten professional seasons, Tom quickly decided that his chances of remaining an Oriole would be greatly enhanced if he could fill in behind the plate.

Shopay recalled the opportunity. "They traded Etchebarren and Jim Frey, one of our coaches, said, 'What do you think about catching?' A day or so later, Earl [Weaver] asked me if I wouldn't mind catching."

And so, for the past few weeks, Tom Shopay has been catching batting practice and warming up Baltimore pitchers in the bullpen—anything to be of some help.

Actually, Shopay hadn't even expected to be with the Orioles this year, not after spending the past two summers with Rochester and reporting to this season's spring training as a non-roster player. "I've been in the International League so long," he said in reference to his nearly six seasons in the Triple-A circuit, "that I should have a pension there."

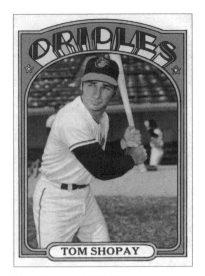

Tom Shopay. *1972 Topps.*

Life in the International League really isn't so bad for a veteran. The salary range for players with Shopay's length of service is from $12,000 to $15,000, and meal money was increased this year to $10 per diem. The caliber of play is, as often as not, equal to that found in a major league ballpark.

But once you've been at the top—and Shopay has two seasons with Baltimore and portions of two others with the Yankees under his belt—it is difficult to settle for less.

"It was really questionable," Shopay related. "I was ready to retire after this year. But I broke camp with Baltimore and, except for a brief period in April, when they couldn't trade Earl Williams, I've been with the club ever since."

As in 1971 and '72, which he spent with the Orioles, the thirty-year-old Shopay has been a handy guy to have around. He's available as a left-handed pinch-hitter, pinch-runner (he's swiped two bases) or spare outfielder. The other night in Boston, Weaver gave him a start in center field. And now he can catch in an emergency.

If the Shopay numbers aren't especially awe inspiring—three hits in twenty at-bats for a .150 average—the Orioles find his versatility of inestimable value.

A lot of the Orioles' numbers haven't been particularly noteworthy this year—ample reason for the club's surprisingly dismal start and still sub-.500 standing. Business, one can gather, is beginning to pick up, though. Including yesterday's 5–2 triumph over the Yankees, the club has won eight of its last ten games and now trails Boston and Milwaukee, the Eastern Division leaders, by four games.

"We just had a slow start. In spring training we were scoring seven, eight runs a game," Shopay said. "When we started the season, we thought nobody was going to stop us and then we got eight games behind."

A lot of the Orioles, Shopay among them, credit Weaver with holding the club together in the face of adversity. The dandy little manager, who, in the history of baseball, trails only the legendary Joe McCarthy in winning percentage, kept the bottom from falling out by refusing to panic.

"He kept morale up," Shopay explained. "He kept telling us we were the best team in the American League."

And now that Don Baylor, Lee May ("He's the type of ballplayer who can carry a team for a month," Shopay noted) and some of the other Orioles have started making regular contact, Weaver's words ring with truth.

Which team do most of the others fear? "The talk in the clubhouses, among players and writers, is the Orioles," said Tom Shopay, smallest major league catcher.

Waterbury Republican, July 6, 1975.

VALENTINE'S FUTURE IS RIGHT NOW

ST. PETERSBURG, Florida—For Bobby Valentine, the future is right now, this spring. Any tomorrows are liable to be spent as a utility player, bouncing from club to club, unless he convinces the Mets hierarchy that he can play second base regularly.

Robert John Valentine, born optimist, believes he will meet the challenge. "I've been the player of the year wherever I've played…in winter ball, the minor leagues, in high school," the dark-haired Stamford native said. "I've done it everywhere except in the big leagues, but if I play up to my capabilities, I can do it here, too."

BOBBY VALENTINE

Bobby Valentine. *1978 Topps.*

Understand, Bobby Valentine never has hit higher than .274 in either of baseball's Major Leagues, nor has he been permitted—by managers or fate—to play a full season.

"That's why this year is so big for me," he continued. "I'm not going to come to spring training next year and be given an opportunity to play every day. Sure, I could stay in the big leagues another six, seven years as a utility player, but that's not really playing the game."

Interviews with Twenty-five of the Nutmeg State's Best

Playing the game means playing every day. At the moment, Valentine is one game-winning home run and 297 percentage points ahead of Doug Flynn in their debate over second base. This is large-scale improvement, for Valentine arrived without promise or fanfare.

To fully appreciate Valentine's progress, you've got to understand where he's coming from. Here is a man with a medical record that far surpasses his baseball accomplishments. Fractured cheekbone, broken nose, double fracture of the right leg, separated shoulder, surgery last winter on his right ankle for removal of bone spurs—this is the Valentine litany, and he is not yet twenty-eight years old.

It would be enough to get a man down. At age twenty, he was the batting champion (.340) and Most Valuable Player of the Triple-A Pacific Coast League, a shortstop with the Dodger organization at his feet. But injuries, coupled with managers who did not fully appreciate his ability (the Dodgers' Walter Alston and Dick Williams of the Angels), coupled with more injuries, have led to this: the Final Chance.

Valentine's road back began with a meeting with Mets Manager Joe Torre. "He made me aware I had no chance of winning the shortstop job," Bobby explained, "but he said there was a chance at second, although we weren't starting even. I had to go out and win the job."

The competition, the aforementioned Flynn, had two advantages: greater range and his acquisition in the controversial Tom Seaver trade. To help justify that transaction, Torre handed Flynn the job before the first ground ball.

Valentine, who spurned numerous scholarship offers—"I received letters from maybe 175 schools"—to play college football, began the spring by playing in "B" games, "the only place I had a chance to show what I could do." He proceeded to collect six hits in seven at-bats, or something equally surrealistic, and moved up to the varsity.

With the Mets, the former Rippowam High athlete is four for ten thus far, which computes to a .400 average in any language. Hit number four was the most memorable by far—Wednesday night's dramatic ninth-inning, two-run home run off the Reds' Doug Bair, turning defeat into a 2–1 New York victory.

"Joe Torre had as much to do with it as anybody," Valentine said. "He set it up with the bunt; he worked the count for me to two balls, no strikes. The opposition had to think we were trying to get the runner over. It's a risky situation for the manager. If I had hit the hell out of the ball to the shortstop, it's a double play."

The Mets' prospects of a division title, if you listen to the "experts," are rather slim. Slimmer than slim? Bobby Valentine, supreme optimist, foresees a better immediate future.

"There are problems," he reasons. "Our pitching is gone, inexperienced. We lack power. Our outfield isn't as strong defensively. We could get into a losing type of syndrome; we've got to stop it before it spreads. Joe Torre's not the type of guy to say we can win the pennant. He'll look ridiculous if we finish in last place. But if we have a total team effort, where everyone takes responsibility for the wins and losses, if we have guys who play close to their capabilities, we can win the pennant."

Bobby Valentine makes it sound so plausible.

Waterbury Republican, March 24, 1978.

COACH FROM WATERBURY
FINDS TALENT ON THE FARM

It is difficult to catch up with Dave Wallace. Throughout a typical spring and summer, his wanderings take him from coast to coast, logging the air miles of a corporate traveler or a modern-day Willy Loman. If this is San Antonio, Texas, it must be June. If this is Bakersfield, California, it must be July. In spring's early weeks, he may be found in Vero Beach under the rising Florida sun. In the fall, he takes up temporary residence in Mesa, Arizona.

It is the nomadic existence of the Los Angeles Dodgers' minor league pitching coordinator. It is the life of Dave Wallace, a forty-six-year-old native of Waterbury. "Baseball's always been part of my life and this is where I want to be," said Wallace, a pleasant, mustachioed man. "The Dodgers are the best organization in sports. And I have the freedom to come home and take care of my children."

As the guru for the Dodgers' minor league pitchers, it is Wallace who assesses their strengths and their weaknesses; it is Wallace who recommends the most promising candidates for promotion, from Vero Beach or Bakersfield to San Antonio, from Albuquerque to Los Angeles.

In the course of a season, he divides his time among all the Dodger farm clubs, spending nearly a week with each team so that he will have the opportunity to evaluate every starting and relief pitcher. His reports are shipped to the offices at Dodger Stadium for appraisal and discussion.

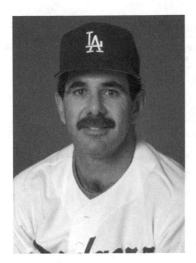

Dave Wallace. *Courtesy of the Los Angeles Dodgers.*

Outside baseball, the name Dave Wallace may elicit little recognition, but those inside the game attest to his expertise.

Orel Hershiser, the Dodgers' most successful pitcher of recent years and winner of the National League's 1988 Cy Young Award, is a Wallace disciple. In his recent book, *Out of the Blue*, Hershiser credited his former minor league coach with detecting a flaw in his delivery that, once corrected, enabled the pitcher to enjoy his greatest major league season. The season was 1988, when Hershiser won twenty-three games, lost eight, broke the major league record with fifty-nine consecutive scoreless innings and pitched the Dodgers to a world championship over the Oakland A's.

"In a way," as Hershiser was quoted in his 1988 "Sportsman of the Year" article in *Sports Illustrated*, "I am the extension of Koufax and Wallace on the mound."

"Orel is wonderful, a down-to-earth guy," Wallace said. "We established a relationship when he was in our minor league system. He's been kind enough to give me some credit."

In thirteen years with the Los Angeles organization, the last six as minor league pitching coordinator, Wallace has contributed to the development of several prominent pitchers. Sid Fernandez and John Franco, both now with the Mets, were early protégées. Wallace helped Bob Welch get squared away when Welch incurred some arm problems during the height of his career. Ramon Martinez, Rick Honeycutt, Tim Belcher and Alex Pena are among other Dodgers, past and present, who have benefited from the coach's counsel and encouragement.

Wallace remembers most of his pupils with some fondness. His voice becomes sad when Tim Crews—the Cleveland relief pitcher who was killed in a boating accident this winter—is mentioned. "I had Tim when he pitched for Albuquerque," Wallace recalled.

David William Wallace once entertained pitching aspirations himself. As a chunky right-hander with a promising fastball, he was a star at Sacred Heart High School in Waterbury and later at the University of New Haven, where he earned a bachelor's degree in business administration.

Signed as a free agent by the Philadelphia Phillies in 1970, he progressed rapidly through their farm system, and by the summer of 1973, he had received his major league baptism with Philadelphia at age twenty-two. If Wallace failed to distinguish himself in four brief appearances that year, he was a participant in an event made for trivia buffs.

On the evening of August 9, 1973, in a game against the San Diego Padres, Dave Wallace was relieved by fellow rookie pitcher Ron Diorio—his former high school and college teammate and a close friend as well. "That's something for *Ripley's Believe it or Not*," says Diorio, forty-seven, today.

For a spell, it seemed that both men from Waterbury would remain with the Phillies, but that wasn't to be. A decade as a professional pitcher brought Wallace little money or glory, just the proverbial cup of coffee on the major league level with the Phillies (1973–74) and the expansion Toronto Blue Jays (1978). The Wallace line in the *Official Encyclopedia of Baseball* reads: "13 games, 0–1 won-lost record, 7.84 earned run average."

"I had marginal ability. I never expected to play eight years in Triple A and almost a year in the big leagues," he said. "I was kind of stuck on Triple A. I wish I had gotten more of a legitimate chance to pitch in the Major Leagues. I probably was a bit wild, didn't throw strikes as consistently as I would have liked."

Ironically, the control would come when it was too late. Activated by Albuquerque during the 1984 and '86 Pacific Coast League seasons, when several pitchers were incapacitated, he pitched well in most of his eight appearances. "I was finally able to get the ball over," he said with a chuckle.

If Wallace were able to alter the course of his baseball career, he might have met Sandy Koufax much earlier than a few years ago. Wallace found Koufax—the Hall of Fame pitcher who threw four no-hitters, won three Cy Young Awards and set several strikeout records—quite willing to share his trade secrets during their springs together as minor league coaches in the Dodgers' Vero Beach training camp.

"I can't believe what this guy knows about pitching. The mechanics and everything else," Wallace said. "In the beginning, I really became a pain in the neck by staying there and asking questions. But Sandy's such a good man. He really understands the human side of the player."

Dave Wallace's goal? He would like to move up to the parent Dodgers as pitching coach, a position that has been held by Ron Perranoski for the past thirteen years. There seems to be job security; prior to Perranoski's arrival, Red Adams and Joe Becker enjoyed similar longevity as tutors of the Dodger pitchers.

"One reason this organization is so special," Wallace had observed some time ago, "is that the big-league guys, [Tom] Lasorda, Perranoski and all the rest, work closely with the minor league managers and coaches. You can learn an awful lot from them."

New York Times, July 11, 1993.

CHAPTER 4

HONORABLE MENTION

Players Who Made Connecticut Their Second Home

One can assemble a powerful all-star team from other players with strong ties to Connecticut—those nonnatives who were raised in the Nutmeg State or who spent a significant portion of their lives here.

We can begin with a pitching staff headed by Hall of Famers Tom Seaver and Ed Walsh, and Smoky Joe Wood, whose outstanding career was truncated by arm injuries. Seaver resided in affluent Greenwich for two decades, beginning when he pitched the New York Mets to two National League pennants and the 1969 World Championship. Walsh, who put forth a remarkable 40–15 record with the Chicago White Sox's 1908 "Hitless Wonders," made Meriden his home for a lengthy period.

Wood, he of the 34–5 record with the 1912 World Champion Boston Red Sox, arrived in New Haven in 1922 to coach Yale baseball. He considered the Elm City home for the remainder of his long life (he died on July 27, 1985, at the age of ninety-five).

Two pitchers with Cy Young Awards, Tom Glavine and David Cone, round out the starting staff on this squad. Both have resided in Greenwich, at least part of the time, in recent years. Glavine is destined for a Hall of Fame plaque.

On the rare occasion when a relief pitcher is needed, we can call upon the Mets' Billy Wagner or former Met Skip Lockwood, both with Greenwich

Top left: Ed Walsh, Meriden. *1911 American Tobacco. Courtesy of the Library of Congress, Prints and Photographs Division.*
Top right: David Cone, Greenwich. *1991 Topps.*
Bottom left: Moe Drabowsky, Windsor. *1968 Topps.*
Bottom right: Jackie Robinson, Stamford. *1949 Bowman.*

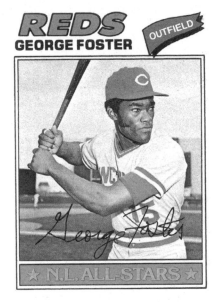

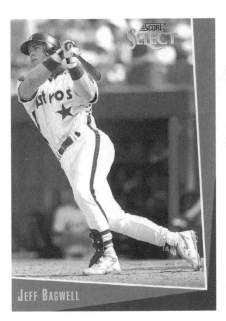

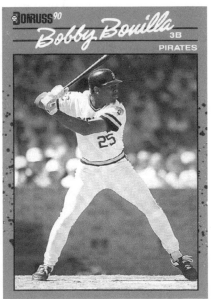

Top left: Willie Upshaw, Fairfield. *1979 Topps.*
Top right: George Foster, Greenwich. *1977 Topps.*
Bottom left: Jeff Bagwell, Killingworth. *1993 Score.*
Bottom right: Bobby Bonilla, Greenwich. *1990 Leaf.*

Lee Mazzilli, Greenwich. *1988 Leaf.*

ties; or the late Moe Drabowsky, who was reared in Windsor after emigrating from Poland.

Let's move to the infield. There's a Hall of Fame second baseman in Jackie Robinson (Stamford) and a probable Hall of Fame first baseman in Jeff Bagwell (Killingworth). Carlos Delgado, the Mets' current first baseman who has amassed more than 430 home runs, recently purchased a home in Greenwich.

The Bronx-born Bobby Bonilla, who is raising his family in Greenwich, will play third base on this mythical team. He was a six-time all-star. This will allow Jumping Joe Dugan—who grew to manhood in Winsted and New Haven—to move from third to shortstop.

The outfield features two potent sluggers who lived in Greenwich, Hall of Famer Ralph Kiner, who won seven home run titles with the Pittsburgh Pirates, and George Foster, whose fifty-two-homer, 149-RBI season in 1977 earned him the Most Valuable Player Award with Cincinnati's Big Red Machine. Fleet Lee Mazzilli, a current Greenwich resident, will put his defensive skills to work as the center fielder.

For pinch-hitters, both Rico Brogna, who was raised in Watertown, and Willie Upshaw, who now makes his home in Fairfield, are available. (Perhaps we can convert one into a left-handed catcher.)

I have interviewed many of these men through the years—indeed, Lockwood was once our houseguest—and three of their stories follow.

A CASUALTY OF THE BASEBALL
STRIKE FINDS A HAVEN

Shirts were playing skins on a wintry afternoon at the Watertown High School gymnasium. Ten freshmen darted up and down the basketball court. Each time a player broke free from a defender, he gestured and shouted for the ball.

"Mike! Mike!" yelled a cutter. "Charlie! Charlie! Bob! Bob!"

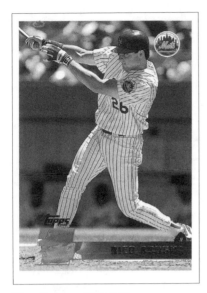

Rico Brogna. *1996 Topps.*

The coach, a broad-shouldered, friendly twenty-four-year-old named Rico Brogna, was visibly annoyed and brought the practice to a momentary halt. "There's too much name-calling out there," he told the players. "That's third-grade stuff. You're in high school now."

The players nodded and, after a few more instructions, resumed their practice. Later, one of the group, Charlie Arrindell, explained what it meant to have a major league first baseman, perhaps Watertown's best-known resident, as their coach.

"You don't really think about it when you're in a game or at practice," he said. "But you tell your family and friends that a Major League baseball player is your coach."

Rico Brogna, rookie first baseman for the New York Mets, is spending the winter of his (and other striking major league players') discontent coaching freshman basketball at his alma mater. The sport is not foreign to him; he coached the squad last year, and basketball was among his sports—although admittedly a distant third behind football and baseball—when he was Watertown High's foremost athlete in the late 1980s.

"I was a guard and a swingman on teams that weren't very successful," Brogna said. "Today, I enjoy giving something back."

As the baseball strike plods through its sixth month, with no signs of a settlement, he speaks about it without anger. "This summer, as well as it went, and getting a chance to play with the Mets, was special to me," Brogna said. Dallas Green, the manager, "gave me an opportunity to play, an opportunity to play against left-handers. After a while, it helped me against righties. He gave me the confidence. I'll have to admit things became a little overwhelming," he added. "It was nice to come back home with my wife and enjoy some time with my parents. I like quiet time."

When the players' strike began on August 12, Brogna was in the process of proving to the Mets and to himself that he belonged in the big leagues. After being recalled from the Mets' farm club at Norfolk, Virginia, on

June 20, he was hitting .351, with an abundance of extra-base hits. On July 25, he collected five hits in as many at-bats, becoming just the third Mets rookie to have that many hits in a game (John Milner in 1972 and Dick Smith in 1964 were the others). In the field, he committed just one error in 336 chances at first base for a fielding percentage of .997.

Brogna's strong performance, although limited to thirty-nine games in the final third of a shortened season, placed him among the National League's finest hitters. Only two players had higher batting averages: a fellow Connecticut product, Jeff Bagwell, formerly of Killingworth, who hit .368 for the Houston Astros and won the Most Valuable Player Award, and Tony Gwynn of the San Diego Padres, who was flirting with a .400 average when the strike arrived and who finished at .394.

People in Watertown had little doubt that their adopted native son would succeed at the game's highest level. (Brogna was born in Turner's Falls, Massachusetts, but arrived in town at the age of seven when his father, Joseph, accepted a teaching position at the Taft School.)

"At every game, you'll see people there from Watertown," said Brogna's mother, Lucille. "One time we bumped into five of his friends from high school in the parking lot."

One resident, Joe Romano, organized a Rico Brogna fan club and led one of the bus trips to Shea Stadium to watch Brogna play.

Roger Ouellette, who coached the Watertown High baseball team during Brogna's senior year—when he batted over .600 and won all of his games as a combination first baseman–pitcher—never doubted for a moment. "Anything he does doesn't amaze me," Ouellette said. "The work ethic, the talent…the kid's the whole package. I have three children at home and I hope they all grow up to be like him."

In high school, Brogna's prodigious skills as an all-state quarterback and seemingly unerring placekicker suggested a career in football. College scouts witnessed an athlete capable of kicking ninety-one straight extra points and setting a Connecticut high school record with a fifty-four-yard field goal. They saw a quarterback who directed Watertown to its first Class S state title in 1986, amassing six thousand career passing yards in the process.

Many colleges beckoned, and Brogna ultimately signed a letter of intent to attend Clemson. "I would have gone there if the Detroit Tigers hadn't made me their number one pick in the baseball draft," he said.

His six seasons in the Detroit farm system, 1988 to 1993, produced solid, but not wonderful, results, and Brogna began to wonder when he would reach the major leagues. Cecil Fielder was firmly entrenched at first base in Detroit. The trade to the Mets last March, for Alan Zinter, could not have been more beneficial.

"The Tigers get so much production out of Cecil, they didn't need another first baseman," Brogna said. "I had a good experience with the Tigers, but it was time to move on. There was no room for promotion."

He continues to savor his moment of success during a nine-game trial with the Tigers in 1992: his first major league home run, against the Yankees' Melido Perez at Tiger Stadium. "Just unbelievable, it's still hard to describe even now," Brogna said, smiling. "The Tiger radio announcer gave me the tape after the game. You can hear the solid whack of the wood."

This winter the promise of bat meeting ball seems remote. The strike drags on and Brogna, who earned the major league minimum salary, a prorated $109,000, in 1994, watches and waits like the Ken Griffeys and Roger Clemenses. He seemed reluctant to discuss the salary cap and other issues, but said, "They're trying to help the younger players…what they're trying to do is benefit us. I know I wouldn't cross a picket line. I would wait it out like everyone else."

New York Times, January 22, 1995.

YES SIR, 1927 YANKEES THE GREATEST

NEW YORK—Were the 1927 New York Yankees the greatest team to walk the face of this earth? Jumping Joe Dugan, with pardonable pride, says it couldn't be anyone else.

"Certainly," said the man who played a sparkling third base for the team they called Murderer's Row. "Who the hell was going to beat them? Not the Big Red Machine. They were a hell-raising team, breaking every rule in the book—starting with Ruth—but they kept winning. The Athletics couldn't catch us."

Joseph Anthony Dugan is eighty years old, and by his own admission, not in the best of health, but his mind is keen and his memory incredibly accurate. And he likes to laugh and make small jokes. "I work for the Red Sox now in public relations. Now ask me what I do."

All right, what do you do?

"Nothing. Not a gosh darn thing."

Jumping Joe Dugan. *Courtesy of the National Baseball Hall of Fame, Cooperstown, New York.*

Yesterday, Dugan and the three other surviving members of the 1927 Yankees—pitchers Waite Hoyt and Bob Shawkey and utility infielder Mike Gazella—returned to Yankee Stadium for the Yankees' thirty-first annual Old Timers Day. The theme for the occasion, appropriate enough, was the fiftieth anniversary of that world championship team.

When Dugan was introduced and began a walking trot onto the field, his mini leap in midstride elicited chuckles from the vast crowd.

Were the 1927 Yankees the greatest? Some numbers, please. They won 110 games and lost just 44. They captured the American League pennant by a whopping 19 games. They batted an aggregate .307 and walloped the then-astounding total of 158 home runs. In the World Series, they blitzed the Pittsburgh Pirates in four straight games. Five of their number—the incomparable Babe Ruth, Lou Gehrig, pitcher Herb Pennock, center fielder Earle Combs and Hoyt—are enshrined in the Baseball Hall of Fame.

"Great hitters. You'll never see the likes of those two again," Dugan said of the Babe and Larruping Lou. "Ruth was wonderful, the best that ever lived. Why shouldn't they love him? He doubled everybody's salary. He was a great outfielder. He could throw. He could run. And he could pitch, don't forget that."

Dugan remembers Gehrig, the powerful, but ill-fated, Iron Horse, as a man with "no charisma, no color. The phlegmatic Dutchman. But," Dugan said, "he was almost as good as Ruth as a hitter, maybe better."

The record books tell us that Ruth complemented his record-setting sixty home runs with 164 runs batted in and a .356 average in that memorable season. Nice. Very nice. But Gehrig did better overall and was voted Most Valuable Player. He led both leagues with 175 RBIs, 447 total bases and fifty-two doubles, batted a lusty .373 and ranked second in the league with forty-seven homers.

On this powerhouse of a team, Dugan, a lifetime .280 hitter, usually found himself in the seventh spot in the batting order.

When pressed, Dugan will admit that a few teams approached the '27 Yankees in ability. The Shoeless Joe Jackson–Eddie Cicotte White Sox of 1917. The Foxx-Simmons-Grove-Cochrane Philadelphia Athletics of 1929–31. The Brooklyn Dodgers of the late 1940s and early 1950s. But approach is the word.

"Look at what we had. I don't believe the other teams were as good."

Joe Dugan's extensive Connecticut background is well-known to graybeards; many still think of him as a state native. He isn't. He was born in Mahanoy City, Pennsylvania, on May 12, 1897.

"When I was fifteen months old, we moved to Winsted. My old man worked for the railroad. We lived there until I graduated from St. Anthony's School. And then we moved to New Haven."

Dugan attended New Haven High School (the forerunner of Hillhouse) and then went on to Holy Cross before signing a bonus contract with the Athletics in 1917. The bonus was the sum of $500.

It was while in the employ of the A's that Dugan acquired the nickname "Jumping Joe." Contrary to popular belief, it wasn't for any acrobatics at the hot corner, but rather due to his penchant for leaving the club.

Dugan remembers the A's owner-manager, Connie Mack, as a "nice man" who "didn't have any money." Mack eventually dealt the third baseman to the Red Sox in January 1922; in late July, Boston traded him to the Yankees.

By 1927, Dugan had already played in three World Series, owned a home in fashionable Scarsdale, had seen his salary increase to $12,000 and was generally acknowledged as the league's premier third baseman.

On the team known as Murderer's Row, though, Joe Dugan was a mere accessory to the fact. He contributed just two home runs and a .269 average. "But I hit good enough. I hit .280 for fourteen years," he reasons. "And I could field. My biggest World Series share was $6,100, $6,200," he said. "I was getting $12,000 [a year]. What's the matter with $18,000?"

In 1927, absolutely nothing.

Did those Yankees, as legend persists, really psyche out the Pirates with an awesome display of distance hitting prior to the World Series? Dugan insists they did.

He remembers waiting his turn in the batting cage, with "the two Waners standing next to me," as Ruth, Gehrig, Tony Lazzeri and the rest drove ball after ball into the stands.

"Holy God," he recalls one of the Waner brothers saying, "do we have to play those birds?"

Unfortunately, they did.

Waterbury Republican, August 4, 1977.

SPORTS SPOTLIGHT: SMOKY JOE WOOD

There are only three pitchers alive who have won thirty or more games in a Major League Baseball season, and New Haven can claim one as a resident, if not as a native. He's Smoky Joe Wood, who fastballed his way to a 34–5 record with the World Champion Boston Red Sox of 1912. Wood is in pretty heady company, since the others are Hall of Famers Lefty Grove (31–4 in 1931) and Dizzy Dean (30–7 in 1934).

Wood and his wife, Laura, live in a comfortable home on Marvel Road, a pretty tree-lined street in the Westville section. They've been out of the limelight for some time, and they like it that way.

Much of their summers are spent on the family farm in Shohola, Pennsylvania, a hamlet in the northeast corner of the Keystone State. Winters, they're here, and have been since 1922.

Smoky Joe Wood and his close friend, Tris Speaker, share this American Tobacco card, circa 1911. *Courtesy of the Library of Congress, Prints and Photographs Division.*

Honorable Mention

"I came here that year to coach Yale freshman baseball," said Wood, whose seventy-six years are belied by a youthful frame and consistent golf scores in the high seventies and low eighties. "I came here with the understanding that I would coach the varsity the next year."

Wood understood correctly. He moved up to the Eli varsity and stayed on until 1942, when another former major leaguer of considerable ability, Red Rolfe, took over. (His career record was 283–228–1.)

Several athletes of note—Albie Booth, for one—came under Wood's tutelage at Yale, including the coach's oldest son, Joe Jr. Perhaps Wood's proudest day was when his Yale team, with young Joe in the lineup, played Colgate, which had sons Steve and Bob Wood on its squad.

"Steve was the best athlete of the three," said Wood, "but he hurt his arm in World War II. He was a left-handed first baseman."

A daughter, Virginia, now the wife of C.M. Whitney, a New Haven realtor, completes the Wood lineup.

Joe Wood is a man of stability. Same wife for fifty-three years, same house for twenty-seven, the same hobbies for a lifetime—golf, hunting and fishing. If his right arm had been as stable, a plaque bearing his likeness would be hanging in the Baseball Hall of Fame at Cooperstown, New York. He was that good.

Smoky Joe—he acquired the nickname from the velocity of his fastball—had a season in 1912 that others only dream about. The five-foot-eleven, 180-pounder set a Red Sox record with those thirty-four wins, produced the highest winning percentage (.872), broke the team strikeout record with 258, pitched ten shutouts and tied the American League mark with sixteen straight victories.

The remarkable thing about Wood's streak is that it ran concurrently with a string of similar proportions by the immortal Walter Johnson, who would win thirty-three games for the Washington Senators that season. Walter's streak began on July 3; Wood's five days later.

The most eventful game of Wood's streak was his pitching duel with Johnson on September 6. Walter's string had ended, but there was a standing-room-only crowd at Fenway Park—in its inaugural year—for the matchup.

"The papers gave the game a tremendous buildup," Wood said with a grin. "They compared our biceps and triceps along with our records."

Wood pitched a corker that day, winning a 1–0 decision. His streak ended fourteen days later in a 6–4 loss at Detroit.

Wood and his wife, Laura, in their living room on Marvel Road in New Haven, 1966. *Mel Tyler photo*.

"We had the pennant clinched so Manager Jake Stahl had the substitutes in," explained Wood. "It was a late inning and the Tigers loaded the bases. Somebody hit a popup to our shortstop—Martin Krug—and it came down and hit him in the belly. All three runs scored and we never could catch up."

Wood capped his memorable year by winning three games—including the clincher—in the World Series against the New York Giants of John McGraw.

If the Chalmers Most Valuable Player Award didn't go to Wood, at least it stayed in the same room. Hall of Fame center fielder Tris Speaker, Joe's road roommate for his entire career, won the award with a .383 batting average, 222 hits, 136 runs scored and ten home runs, which tied for the league lead.

"Tris was probably my finest friend in baseball," said Wood. "He was the greatest outfielder I've ever seen."

At age twenty-two, Smoky Joe Wood was baseball's number one pitcher, with untold heights still to scale. Within three years, his pitching career was over, and he was forced to switch to the outfield.

Honorable Mention

As Wood tells it: "I broke my thumb in Detroit early in 1913 and missed about two months. I don't know whether I returned too soon, but I never was the same pitcher again."

Boston won another championship in 1915, and Wood had enough smoke left to bag the league earned run average title with 1.49. But a sore arm prevented him from pitching in the Series against the Philadelphia Phillies, and he sat out all of 1916.

At the urging of Speaker, now the Cleveland center fielder, the Indians purchased Wood's contract the following year and placed him in the outfield. He played five seasons for the Indians, won a World Series with them in 1920 and retired two years later following a year in which he batted .297 and drove in ninety-two runs.

"I was pretty well up there as a pitcher," said Wood, "but I was just another ballplayer as an outfielder."

Mediocrity wasn't for Joe Wood.

Several months after this column appeared in the *New Haven Journal-Courier*, I had the privilege of presenting the Connecticut Sports Writers' Alliance's most coveted award, the Gold Key, to Smoky Joe Wood at the organization's annual dinner in Hartford. If memory serves, Mickey Mantle was among those on the dais that evening. Shortly after I rejoined the Society for American Baseball Research (SABR) in 2005, I became affiliated with one of its Connecticut arms—the chapter named for Smoky Joe Wood.

New Haven Journal-Courier, 1966.

CHAPTER 5

THEY ALSO SERVE

Umpires

W here would the game of baseball be without the umpires? Even Earl Weaver, the late Billy Martin and other managers known for their belligerence toward the men in blue would admit, perhaps with reluctance, that the game would be reduced to a state of chaos without their presence. They enforce the rules, (try to) keep the peace and make difficult judgment calls within milliseconds on a daily basis. They are vital to the game's integrity.

Connecticut has contributed several of its native sons to this honorable profession. Among the most prominent are the still-active John Hirschbeck (Stratford), Dan Iassogna (Bridgeport) and Ed Rapuano (New Haven), as well as the retired Terry Tata (Waterbury), Mark Hirschbeck (Stratford), Greg Kosc (Bridgeport) and the late Frank Dascoli (Danielson). Mark, the younger of the Hirschbeck brothers, was forced into retirement in 2004 following multiple hip replacement surgeries.

Tata's late stepfather, Augie Guglielmo, was a National League umpire during the 1952 season, but he spent the bulk of his career in the Triple-A International League. Which reminds me of this quote from Guglielmo in a 1979 interview: "Dan Parker once wrote that if he was being tried for murder, he'd want twelve umpires as his jury."

During my tenure in Waterbury, I interviewed Terry Tata on dozens of occasions and, in 1973, was among the speakers at his bachelor dinner. When I became ill during the 1979 World Series, he made a welcome visit to my hotel room. Here is more about the man.

AN UMPIRE'S ROAD TO THE BIG LEAGUES

America's eyes—at least those still partly open at this late hour on an October evening—were riveted on television screens. Mark Lemke of the Atlanta Braves raced toward home plate as the Minnesota Twins' mustachioed catcher, Brian Harper, awaited the throw.

Both ball and runner appeared to arrive simultaneously. The Braves' second baseman slid past the catcher, who seemed to tag him out as the two made brief contact.

"Safe!" signaled the man, Terry Tata, closest to the autumnal tableau. "Safe!" signaled the plate umpire once again. Harper, a bear of a man at six feet, two inches tall and perhaps 210 pounds, appeared ready to fly into a rage. But a potentially sticky scene was averted when the Twins realized the contact point had been the catcher's elbow; the ball had not touched the baserunner's jersey.

Thanks to Tata's correct split-second decision, Americans could turn off their television sets. Lemke's run with two outs in the bottom of the ninth inning had given the Braves a 3–2 victory in the fourth game of the 1991 World Series.

"NICE CALL"

Terry Tata, Waterbury. *1988 T&M Sports.*

"Tim McCarver was very generous with his comments that night," the umpire, a fifty-two-year-old native of Waterbury, recalled early this summer. "Writers and photographers were coming by and saying, 'Nice call.' That was the most memorable play in the 1991 Series, and I had a whole winter to enjoy it."

Even Commissioner Fay Vincent voiced a positive comment. "My hero!" he told Tata, only partly in jest, after the game.

Presumably, few baseball fans would share the commissioner's assessment of Tata or, for that matter, describe any umpire in such a manner. An umpire is just there, merely tolerated, in view but unseen, until forced to render a decision that incenses one side or the other. And then the arguments begin.

But Tata seems to enjoy his profession. He is in his twentieth year in the National League and his thirty-third season as an umpire in professional baseball. In seniority and prestige, he ranks high among his peers. He is the chief of his four-man crew.

TAUNTS AND ARGUMENTS

Tata, who wears number nineteen, endures occasional taunts and profanity from fans and infrequent arguments with managers and players. His annual salary is around $135,000 and he earns $6,000 as crew chief and a per diem of $190 when he is on the road.

When he is selected to work in a World Series, which has happened three times (1979, 1987 and last year), or in the National League Championship Series (five such assignments) or Major League All-Star Game (two thus far), there is further remuneration. "I've always loved baseball," he said, "and umpiring has given me a good life."

A job few thin-skinned people would choose has enabled Terry and Janice Tata to live in a four-bedroom Colonial-style house in Cheshire, with a wine cellar, and a silver Mercedes parked in the driveway. Mrs. Tata, who took early retirement from her teaching career in the Waterbury school system, occasionally accompanies her husband on road trips.

Life was not always so comfortable for Tata. At the age of sixteen, Terry Anthony Tata became a high school dropout and seemed to be on a dead-end path. "I quit Crosby as a sophomore, he said. "I didn't realize the importance of an education." And so he worked at Lux Clock, Benrus and other factories in the city in which he was born.

Given an opportunity to umpire in Waterbury's public and parochial school leagues, Tata found himself enjoying his work for the first time. "I got seventy-five cents from each coach; the next year they doubled it," he said with a laugh.

In the winter of 1960, Tata became serious about the work and enrolled at the Al Somers Umpiring School in Daytona Beach, Florida. That spring, at nineteen, he was placed in the Midwest League, at Class D, the lowest rung on the ladder.

Encouragement came from the man who became his stepfather, Angelo "Augie" Guglielmo, a professional umpire for twenty years and a member of the National League staff in 1952. "I always knew Terry had what it took to make it," said Guglielmo, who is about to celebrate his eightieth birthday in his native Waterbury.

Shortly after his professional debut, Tata appeared on the television game show, *What's My Line?* He discovered that he enjoyed the limelight. "I was supposed to have been the youngest umpire in professional baseball," recalled Tata, whose boyish looks made him appear even younger. "I went around the panel once before somebody—I think it was Arlene Francis—guessed what I did."

Tata toiled in the game's outposts for thirteen years, from the Midwest League to the Northern League, from the heat and humidity of the Texas League to the larger, but nonetheless minor league cities of the International League. He supplemented a modest income by working for an airport limousine service during the winters.

Finally, in the spring of 1973, Tata was promoted to the National League, where the starting salary was $12,500. Since then, he has enjoyed a progressively better life that includes first-class hotels and meals, cross-country jet travel and better working conditions. In recent years, umpires have begun to receive two and three weeks' vacation during the playing season.

"It's easier in the big leagues; in most games, the pitchers are around the plate," he said. "But there's more pressure, too. There's more at stake. You hear the fans, but you don't let them get to you."

Sometimes he is unable to tune out the players. Willie McCovey, the San Francisco Giants first baseman who is now enshrined in the Baseball Hall of Fame, was Tata's first ejection from a National League game. In disputing a strikeout, the Giants' slugger used profanity, which the umpires' code forbids. In most years, Tata rarely ejects more than two or three players.

His stock among his peers is gaining recognition. Last winter, Tata received the Major League Umpire of the Year award in Florida, where his excellent work in the World Series was cited.

"He had every tough call imaginable," said Harry Wendelstedt, who operates the school for umpires where the award was presented. "I think he set a standard."

People in Waterbury are proud of Terry Tata's accomplishments. Next month he is to be inducted into the Hank O'Donnell Hall of Fame, named for the late local sports editor, at Municipal Stadium.

And each winter, on visits to the city's schools, he reminds children about the importance of an education. "Stay in school," he tells them. "Don't do what I did."

New York Times, July 26, 1992.

APPENDIX

RECORDS

- All-Time Roster of Connecticut Major Leaguers
- Connecticut-born Managers
- Connecticut High Schools' Alumni in Major Leagues
- Connecticut Colleges' Alumni in Major Leagues
- Connecticut Natives in the Baseball Hall of Fame
- World Series Participants
- All-Star Game Participants
- Award Winners
- League Leaders
- Outstanding Performances
- Single-Season Highs

Player	Birthplace	DOB	High School	Died	Pos	Years	Average/W-L
Hezekiah Allen	Westport	2/25/1863		9/21/1916	C	1884	.667
Pete Appleton	Terryville	5/20/1904	Terryville	1/18/1974	P	1927–28, '30–33, '36–42, '45	57–66
Brad Ausmus	**New Haven**	**4/14/1969**	**Cheshire**		**C**	**1993–**	**.252**
Howard Baker	Bridgeport	3/1/1888		1/16/1964	3B	1912, '14–15	.220
Jack Barry	Meriden	4/26/1887	Meriden	4/23/1961	SS/2B	1908–19	.243
Bob Barthelson	New Haven	7/15/1924	Hillhouse	4/14/2000	P	1944	1–1
Ed Beecher	Guilford	7/2/1860		9/12/1935	OF	1887, '89–91	.273
Zeke Bella	Greenwich	8/23/1930	Greenwich		OF	1957, '59	.196
Steve Blass	Canaan	4/18/1942	Housatonic		P	1964, '66–74	103–76
Bruce Boisclair	Putnam	12/9/1952	Killingly		OF	1974, '76–79	.263
George Bone	New Haven	8/28/1874		5/26/1918	SS	1901	.302
Ricky Bottalico	New Britain	8/26/1969	South Catholic		P	1994–05	33–42
Emmons "Chick" Bowen	New Haven	7/26/1897	Hillhouse	8/9/1948	OF	1919	.200
Darren Bragg	Waterbury	9/7/1969	Taft		OF	1994–2004	.255
Craig Breslow	**New Haven**	**8/8/1980**	**Trumbull**		**P**	**2005–06, '08–**	**0–2**
Herman Bronkie	S. Manchester	3/31/1885		5/27/1968	3B/2B	1910–12, '14, '18–19, '22	.242
George Bryant	Bridgeport	2/10/1857		3/14/1898	2B	1885	.000
John Caneira	Waterbury	10/7/1952	Naugatuck		P	1977–78	2–2
Jesse Carlson	**New Britain**	**12/31/1980**	**Berlin**		**P**	**2008–**	

Records

Player	Birthplace	DOB	High School	Died	Pos	Years	Average/W-L
Pete Castiglione	Greenwich	2/13/1921	Greenwich		IF	1947–54	.255
Art Ceccarelli	New Haven	4/2/1930	West Haven		P	1955–57, '59–60	9–18
Scott Chiasson	Norwich	8/14/1977	Norwich Free Academy		P	2001–02	1–1
Roy "Pepper" Clark	New Haven	5/11/1874		11/1/1925	OF	1902	.145
Al "Lefty" Clauss	New Haven	6/24/1891		9/13/1952	P	1913	0–1
Joe Connor	Waterbury	12/8/1874		11/8/1857	C/IF	1895, '00–01, '05	.199
*Roger Connor	Waterbury	7/1/1857		1/4/1919	1B	1880–97	.317
Joe Conzelman	Bristol	7/4/1885		4/17/1979	P	1913–15	6–8
Tommy Corcoran	New Haven	1/4/1869		6/25/1960	SS/2B	1890–07	.256
Ed Cotter	Hartford	7/4/1904		6/14/1959	SS/3B	1926	.308
Ed Coughlin	Hartford	8/5/1861		12/25/1952	P/OF	1884	.250
Morrie Critchley	New London	3/26/1850		3/6/1910	P	1882	1–4
George Curry	Bridgeport	12/21/1888		10/5/1963	P	1911	0–3
Jud Daley	S. Coventry	3/4/1884		1/26/1967	OF	1911–12	.250
George "Kiddo" Davis	Bridgeport	2/12/1902	Bgt. Central	3/4/1983	OF	1926, '32–38	.282
Rajai Davis	Norwich	10/19/1980	New London		OF	2006–	.270
Bill Dawley	Norwich	2/6/1958	Griswold		P	1983–89	27–30
Brian Dayett	New London	1/22/1957	Valley Regional		OF	1983–87	.258
Mark DeJohn	Middletown	9/18/1953	Wdrw. Wilson		IF	1982	.190
Bill Denehy	Middletown	3/31/1946	Wdrw. Wilson		P	1967–68, '71	1–10
Chris Denorfia	Bristol	7/15/1980	Choate		OF	2005–06, '08–	.278

PLAYER	BIRTHPLACE	DOB	HIGH SCHOOL	DIED	POS	YEARS	AVERAGE/ W-L
Rob Dibble	Bridgeport	1/24/1964	Southington		P	1988–93, '95	27–25
Ron Diorio	Waterbury	7/15/1946	Sacred Heart		P	1973–74	0–0
Red Donahue	Waterbury	1/23/1873		8/25/1913	P	1893, '95–06	166–175
Jim Donnelly	New Haven	7/19/1865		3/15/1915	2B/SS/ OF	1884–91, '96–98	.229
Jerry Dorgan	Meriden	1856		6/10/1891	OF/C	1880–82, '84–85	.282
Mike Dorgan	Middletown	10/2/1853		4/26/1909	OF/IF/ C/P	1877–81, '83–87, 1890	.274
Walt Dropo	Moosup	1/30/1923	Plainfield		1B	1949–61	.270
Walt "Monk" Dubiel	Hartford	2/12/1918	Hartford Public	10/23/1969	P	1944–45, '48–52	45–53
George Dunlop	Meriden	7/19/1888		12/12/1972	SS/3B	1913–14	.200
Jayson Durocher	Hartford	8/18/1974	Scottsdale, AZ		P	2002–03	3–1
Angel Echevarria	Bridgeport	5/25/1971	Bassick		OF	1996–2002	.280
Jim Egan	Derby	1858		9/26/1884	OF/P/C	1882	.200
Johnny Ellis	New London	8/21/1948	East Lyme		1B/C	1969–81	.262
George Enright	New Britain	5/9/1954			C	1976	.000
Pete Falsey	New Haven	4/24/1891		5/23/1976	PH	1914	.000
Bill Farrell	Bridgeport	N/A		Dec.	OF/C/SS	1882–83	.143
Ray Foley	Naugatuck	6/23/1906		3/22/1980	PH	1928	.000
Hod Ford	New Haven	7/23/1897	Somerville, MA	1/29/1977	SS/2B	1919–33	.263
Brook Fordyce	New London	5/7/1970	St. Bernard		C	1995–2004	.258

Player	Birthplace	DOB	High School	Died	Pos	Years	Average/ W-L
Clarence "Pop" Foster	New Haven	4/8/1878		4/16/1944	OF/IF	1898–1901	.281
Bill Gannon	New Haven	3/17/1873		4/26/1927	OF/P	1898, '01	.148
Billy Gardner	Waterford	7/19/1927			IF	1954–63	.237
Pete Gilbert	Baltic	9/6/1867		1/1/1912	3B	1890–92, '94	.242
Fred Goldsmith	New Haven	5/15/1852		3/28/1939	P/OF/1B	1879–84	112-68
Mauro Gozzo	New Britain	3/7/1966	Berlin		P	1989–94	7–7
Jason Grabowski	New Haven	5/24/1976	Clinton		OF/1B	2002–05	.196
Adam Greenberg	New Haven	2/21/1981	Guilford		PH	2005	.000
Henry Gruber	Hamden	12/14/1863		9/26/1932	P	1887–91	61–78
* Edward "Ned" Hanlon	Montville	8/22/1857		4/14/1937	OF	1880–92	.260
John Hiland	Baltic	9/1/1860		4/30/1901	2B	1885	.000
Danny Hoffman	Canton	3/2/1880		3/14/1922	OF	1903–11	.256
Paul Hopkins	Chester	9/25/1904		1/2/2004	P	1927, '29	1–1
Bill Hutchison	New Haven	12/17/1859		3/19/1926	P	1884, '89–95, '97	184–163
Merwin Jacobson	New Britain	3/7/1894		1/13/1978	OF	1915–16, '26–27	.230
Joey Jay	Middletown	8/15/1935	Wdrw. Wilson		P	1953–66	99–91
Bill Jensen	New Haven	11/23/1888		3/27/1917	P	1912, '14	1–3
Paul Johnson	North Grosvenordale	9/2/1896		2/14/1973	OF	1920–21	.276
Jay Johnstone	Manchester	11/20/1945	West Covina, CA		OF	1966–85	.267
Jack Jones	Litchfield	10/23/1860		10/19/1936	P	1883	11–7

PLAYER	BIRTHPLACE	DOB	HIGH SCHOOL	DIED	POS	YEARS	AVERAGE/ W-L
Ray Keating	Bridgeport	7/21/1893		11/28/1963	P	1912–19	28–51
Jim Keenan	New Haven	2/10/1858		9/21/1926	C/IF/OF	1880, '82, '84–91	.241
Tom Kelley	Manchester	1/5/1944	Manchester		P	1964–67, '71–73	20–22
Kurt Kepshire	Bridgeport	7/3/1959	Bgt. Central		P	1984–86	16–15
Fred Klobedanz	Waterbury	6/13/1871		4/12/1940	P	1896–99, '02	53–25
Nick Koback	Hartford	7/19/1935	Hartford Public		C	1953–55	.121
Larry Kopf	Bristol	11/3/1890		10/15/1986	IF	1913–23	.249
Wally Kopf	Stonington	7/10/1899		4/30/1979	3B	1921	.333
George "Candy" LaChance	Putnam	2/14/1870		8/18/1932	1B/SS/ OF/C	1893–1905	.280
Art "Hi" Ladd	Willimantic	2/9/1870		5/7/1948	OF	1898	.200
Roger LaFrancois	Norwich	8/2/1954	Griswold		C	1982	.400
Joe Lahoud	Danbury	4/14/1947	Abbott Tech		OF	1968–78	.223
John Lamb	Sharon	7/20/1946	Housatonic		P	1970–71, '73	0–2
Tom Leahy	New Haven	6/2/1869		6/11/1951	C/OF/3B	1897–98, '01, '05	.256
Jack Leary	New Haven	7/1857		Dec.	OF/IF/P	1880–84	.232
Jim Lehan	Hartford	5/14/1856		Dec.	IF/OF	1884	.333
Jim Lillie	New Haven	7/27/1861		11/9/1890	OF/P/IF	1883–86	.219
Brian Looney	New Haven	9/26/1969	Cheshire		P	1993–95	0–1
Billy Lush	Bridgeport	11/10/1873		8/28/1951	OF/IF	1895–97, '01–04	.249
Ernie Lush	Bridgeport	11/1/1885		2/26/1937	OF	1910	.000
Pat Maloney	Grosvenordale	1/19/1888		6/27/1979	OF	1912	.215

Records

Player	Birthplace	DOB	High School	Died	Pos	Years	Average/W-L
Dick McAuliffe	Hartford	11/29/1939	Farmington		2B/SS/3B	1960–75	.247
Greg McCarthy	Norwalk	10/30/1968	Bridgeport Central		P	1996–98	2–3
John McDonald	**New London**	**9/24/1974**	**East Lyme**		**IF**	**1999–**	**.240**
Frank "Beauty" McGowan	Branford	11/8/1901		5/6/1982	OF	1922–23, '28–29, '37	.262
Matty McIntyre	Stonington	6/12/1880		4/2/1920	OF	1901, '04–12	.269
Jack McMahon	Waterbury	10/15/1869		12/30/1894	1B/C	1892–93	.243
John Michaels	Bridgeport	7/10/1907	Warren Harding	11/18/1996	P	1932	1–6
Johnny Moore	Waterville	3/23/1902	Crosby	4/4/1991	OF	1928–37, '45	.307
Moe Morhardt	Manchester	1/16/1937	Manchester		1B	1961–62	.206
Kevin Morton	Norwalk	8/3/1968	Brien McMahon		P	1991	6–5
Tim Murnane	Naugatuck	6/4/1852		2/7/1917	1B/OF	1876–78, '84	.258
John Murphy	New Haven	1879		4/20/1949	SS/3B	1902–03	.240
Ed Murray	Mystic	5/8/1895		11/8/1970	SS	1917	.000
Charles Nagy	Bridgeport	5/5/1967	Roger Ludlowe		P	1990–2003	129–105
Phil Nastu	Bridgeport	3/8/1955	Bassick		P	1978–80	3–5
Fred "Tricky" Nichols	Bridgeport	7/26/1850		8/22/1897	P/OF	1876–78, '80, '82	24–44
Al Niemiec	Meriden	5/18/1911		10/29/1995	2B/SS	1934, '36	.200
Art "Ole" Olsen	S. Norwalk	9/12/1894	Norwalk	9/12/1980	P	1922–23	8–7
*Orator Jim O'Rourke	Bridgeport	9/1/1850		1/3/1919	OF/IF/C	1876–93, '04	.310

Player	Birthplace	DOB	High School	Died	Pos	Years	Average/ W-L
John O'Rourke	Bridgeport	8/23/1849		6/23/1911	OF	1879–80, '83	.295
Queenie O'Rourke	Bridgeport	12/26/1883		12/22/1955	OF/IF	1908	.231
John Papa	Bridgeport	12/5/1940	Stratford		P	1961–62	0–0
Tom Parsons	Lakeville	9/13/1939	Housatonic		P	1963–65	2–13
Carl Pavano	New Britain	1/8/1976	Southington		P	1998–2005, '07	62–64
John "Pretzels" Pezzullo	Bridgeport	12/10/1910	Conn. State Tech	5/16/1990	P	1935–36	3–5
Dan Phelan	Thomaston	7/23/1864		12/7/1945	1B	1890	.250
Jimmy Piersall	Waterbury	11/14/1929	Leavenworth		OF/SS	1950, '52–67	.272
Cecil Pillion	Hartford	4/13/1894		9/30/1962	P	1915	0–0
Emil Planeta	Higganum	1/31/1909		2/2/1963	P	1931	0–0
Mike Porzio	Waterbury	8/20/1972	Fairfield Prep		P	1999, '02–03	3–3
Tad Quinn	Torrington	9/25/1881		8/6/1946	P	1902–03	0–1
Mike Raczka	New Britain	11/16/1962	Southington		P	1992	0–0
Joe Regan	Seymour	7/12/1872		11/18/1948	OF	1898	.200
Charlie Reilley	Hartford	1856		11/4/1904	C/OF/IF	1879–82, '84	.210
Mike Robertson	Norwich	10/9/1970	Servite, CA		1B	1996–98	.190
Jim Rogers	Hartford	4/9/1872		1/21/1900	IF	1896–97	.236
Henri Rondeau	Danielson	5/5/1887		5/28/1943	OF/C/1B	1913, '15–16	.206
Ed Rowen	Bridgeport	10/22/1857		2/22/1892	C/OF/IF	1882–84	.242
Mike Sandlock	Old Greenwich	10/17/1915	Wright Tech		C/IF	1942, '44–46, '53	.240

Records

Player	Birthplace	DOB	High School	Died	Pos	Years	Average/ W-L
Jim Savage	Southington	8/29/1883		6/26/1940	OF/IF	1912, '14–15	.276
Bob Saverine	Norwalk	6/2/1941	Darien		IF	1959, '62–67	.239
Ollie Sax	Branford	11/5/1904		3/21/1982	3B	1928	.176
Johnny Scalzi	Stamford	3/22/1907	Stamford	9/27/1962	PH	1931	.000
Freddy Schmidt	Hartford	2/9/1916			P	1944, '46–47	13–11
Dan Shannon	Bridgeport	3/23/1865		10/25/1913	2B/SS	1889–91	.233
Frank "Spec" Shea	Naugatuck	10/2/1920	Naugatuck	7/19/2002	P	1947–49, '51–55	56–46
Biff Sheehan	Hartford	2/13/1868		10/21/1923	OF/1B	1895–96	.302
Jim Sheehan	New Haven	7/3/1913	Hillhouse	12/2/2003	C	1936	.000
Rollie Sheldon	Putnam	12/17/1936	Woodstock Academy		P	1961–62, '64–66	38–36
Tom Shopay	Bristol	2/21/1945	Bristol Eastern		OF/C	1967–72, '75–77	.201
Matt Sinatro	Hartford	3/22/1960	Conard		C	1981–84, '87–92	.190
Edgar Smith	North Haven	10/15/1860		Dec.	OF	1883	.217
George Smith	Byram	5/31/1892	Greenwich	1/7/1965	P	1916–23	41–81
Earl Snyder	New Britain	5/6/1976	Plainville		1B/3B	2002, '04	.203
General Stafford	Thompson	1/30/1868		9/18/1923	P	1890	3–9
Augie Swentor	Seymour	11/21/1899		11/10/1969	C	1922	.000
John Terry	Waterbury	11/1/1879		4/27/1933	P	1902–03	1–2
Dick Tettelbach	New Haven	6/26/1929	Hillhouse	1/26/1995	OF	1955–57	.150
Tim Teufel	Greenwich	7/7/1958	St. Mary's		IF	1983–93	.254
Johnny Tillman	Bridgeport	10/6/1893		4/7/1964	P	1915	1–0

PLAYER	BIRTHPLACE	DOB	HIGH SCHOOL	DIED	POS	YEARS	AVERAGE/ W-L
Bill Tobin	Hartford	10/10/1854		10/10/1912	1B	1880	.158
Tom Tuckey	Union City	10/7/1884		10/17/1950	P	1908–09	3–12
Bobby Valentine	Stamford	5/13/1950	Rippowam		IF/OF	1969, '71–79	.260
Mo Vaughn	Norwalk	12/15/1967	Trinity-Pawling		1B/DH	1991–2003	.293
Dave Wallace	Waterbury	9/7/1947	Sacred Heart		P	1973–74, '78	0–1
Ed Walsh	Meriden	2/11/1905	Meriden	10/31/1937	P	1928–30, '32	11–24
Gary Waslewski	Meriden	7/21/1941	Berlin		P	1967–72	11–26
Eddie Wilson	Hamden	9/7/1909	Hillhouse	4/11/1979	OF	1936–37	.317
Ed Wojna	Bridgeport	8/20/1960	Masuk		P	1985–87, '89	4–10
Walt "Lefty" Wolf	Hartford	6/10/1900		9/25/1971	P	1921	0–0
George Woodend	Hartford	12/9/1917		5/1/1980	P	1944	0–0
George "Pinky" Woods	Waterbury	5/22/1915		10/30/1982	P	1943–45	13–21
Frank Woodward	New Haven	5/17/1894		6/11/1961	P	1918–19, '21–23	9–15
Ron Wotus	Colchester	3/3/1961	Bacon Academy		SS/2B	1983–84	.207
Bill "Ad" Yale	Bristol	4/17/1870		4/27/1948	1B	1905	.077

Bold indicates active in 2008.

Note: Jamie D'Antona, a Greenwich native and graduate of Trumbull High School, was promoted from Triple-A Tucson to the *Arizona Diamondbacks* in July 2008. Birthdate: May 12, 1982. Position: third base.

MANAGERS

MANAGERS	HOMETOWN	YEARS	CLUBS	W-L	PENNANTS
Jack Barry	Meriden	1917	Boston AL	90–62	
*Roger Connor	Waterbury	1896	Buffalo NL	8–37	
Mike Dorgan	Middletown	1879–81	Syracuse, Providence, Worcester NL	67–70	
Billy Gardner	Waterford	1981–85, '87	Minnesota, Kansas City AL	330–417	
* Edward "Ned" Hanlon	Montville	1889–1907	Pittsburgh, Baltimore, Brooklyn, Cincinnati NL	1313–1116	5
Tim Murnane	Naugatuck	1884	Boston UA	58–51	
*Orator Jim O'Rourke	Bridgeport	1881–84, '93	Buffalo, Washington NL	246–258	
Jim Rogers	Hartford	1897	Louisville NL	17–24	
Bob Schaefer	Putnam	1991, 2005	Kansas City AL	6–12	
Dan Shannon	Bridgeport	1889, '91	Louisville, Washington NL	25–80	
Bobby Valentine	Stamford	1985–92, '96–02	Texas AL, New York NL	1172–1072	1

*Indicates Hall of Fame

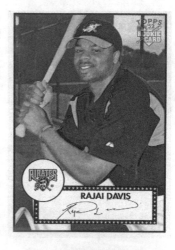

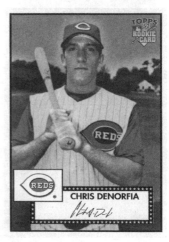

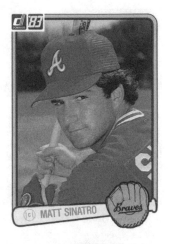

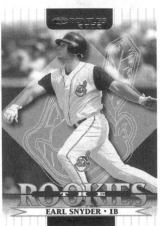

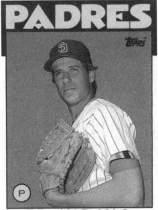

Opposite, clockwise from top left:
Ricky Bottalico. *1995 Topps*;
Rajai Davis. *2007 Topps*; Brian
Dayett. *1985 Topps*; Chris
Denorfia. *2007 Topps*; Scott
Chaisson. *2002 Topps*; Darren
Bragg. *1998 Upper Deck*.

This page, clockwise from top left:
Jay Johnstone. *1981 Topps*;
Matt Sinatro. *1983 Donruss*;
Earl Snyder. *2002 Donruss*;
Ed Wojna. *1986 Topps*; Mike
Raczka. *1993 Score*.

CONNECTICUT HIGH SCHOOLS' ALUMNI IN MAJOR LEAGUES

Abbott Tech, Danbury (1)—Joe Lahoud
Avon Old Farms (1)—Juan Nieves
Bacon Academy, Colchester (1)—Ron Wotus
Bassick, Bridgeport (2)—Angel Echevarria, Phil Nastu
Berlin (3)—Jesse Carlson, Mauro "Goose" Gozzo, Gary Waslewski
Bridgeport Central (3)—George "Kiddo" Davis, Kurt Kepshire, Greg McCarthy
Brien McMahon, Norwalk (1)—Kevin Morton
Bristol Eastern (1)—Tom Shopay
Bulkeley, Hartford (1)—Bob "Spike" Repass
Cheshire (2)—Brad Ausmus, Brian Looney
Choate, Wallingford (1)—Chris Denorfia
Conard, West Hartford (1)—Matt Sinatro
Connecticut State Tech, Bridgeport (1)—John "Pretzels" Pezzullo
Crosby, Waterbury (1)—Johnny Moore
Darien (1)—Bob Saverine
East Lyme (2)—John McDonald, Pete Walker
Fairfield Prep (2)—Matt Merullo, Mike Porzio
Farmington (1)—Dick McAuliffe
Greenwich (3)—Zeke Bella, Pete Castiglione, George Smith
Griswold, Jewett City (2)—Bill Dawley, Roger LaFrancois
Guilford (1)—Adam Greenberg
Hartford Public (2)—Monk Dubiel, Nick Koback
Hillhouse, New Haven (5)—Bob Barthelson, Jumping Joe Dugan, Jim Sheehan, Dick Tettelbach, Eddie Wilson
Housatonic Regional, Falls Village (3)—Steve Blass, John Lamb, Tom Parsons
Joel Barlow, Redding (1)—Charlie Morton
Killingly, Danielson (1)—Bruce Boisclair
Leavenworth, Waterbury (1)—Jim Piersall
Loomis Chaffee, Windsor (4)—Mark Brown, Robert Davis, Moe Drabowsky, Matt Murray
Masuk, Monroe (1)—Ed Wojna
Meriden (2)—Jack Barry, Ed Walsh Jr.
Morgan, Clinton (1)—Jason Grabowski
Naugatuck (2)—John Caneira, Frank "Spec" Shea
New London (2)—Rajai Davis, John Ellis
North Haven (1)—Paul Householder
Norwalk (2)—Kevin Morton, Ole Olsen
Norwich Free Academy (1)—Scott Chiasson

Records

Plainfield (1)—Walt Dropo
Plainville (1)—Earl Snyder
Rippowam, Stamford (1)—Bobby Valentine
Robert E. Fitch, Groton (1)—Paul Menhart
Roger Ludlowe, Fairfield (1)—Charles Nagy
Sacred Heart, Waterbury (2)—Ron Diorio, Dave Wallace
St. Bernard, Uncasville (1)—Brook Fordyce
St. Mary's, Greenwich (1)—Tim Teufel
South Catholic, Hartford (1)—Ricky Bottalico
Southington (4)—Rob Dibble, Carl Pavano, Chris Peterson, Mike Raczka
Stamford (1)—Johnny Scalzi
Stratford (1)—John Papa
Taft, Watertown (1)—Darren Bragg
Terryville (1)—Pete Jablonowski (Appleton)
Trumbull (2)—Craig Breslow, Jamie D'Antona
Valley Regional, Deep River (1)—Brian Dayett
Warren Harding, Bridgeport (2)—George Estock, John Michaels
Watertown (1)—Rico Brogna
West Haven (2)—Art Ceccarelli, Rob Radosyk
Woodrow Wilson, Middletown (3)—Mark DeJohn, Bill Denehy, Jocy Jay
Woodstock Academy (1)—Rollie Sheldon
Wright Tech, Stamford (1)—Mike Sandlock
Xavier, Middletown (1)—Jeff Bagwell

Connecticut Colleges' Alumni in Major Leagues

Bridgeport, University of (3)—Phil Nastu (1973–76), John Papa (1959–60), Dave Wissman (1960–61)
Central Connecticut State University (2)—Ricky Bottalico (1990–91), Skip Jutze (1965–68)
Coast Guard Academy (0)
Connecticut, University of (10)—Jesse Carlson (2000–02), Walt Dropo (1943), Jeff Fulchino, Jason Grabowski (1995–97), Roberto Hernandez (1985), Moe Morhardt (1957–59), Charles Nagy (1987–88), Rollie Sheldon (1960), Pete Walker (1989–90), Gary Waslewski (1960)
Eastern Connecticut State University (2)—John Caneira (1971–74), Scott Chiasson (1996–98)
Fairfield University (1)—Keefe Cato (1977–79)
Hartford, University of (2)—Jeff Bagwell (1987–89), Earl Snyder (1995–98)
Mitchell College (1)—John Ellis
New Haven, University of (10)—Steve Bedrosian (1978), Ron Diorio (1966–69), Cameron Drew (1983–85), Tom Grant (1976–79), Kurt Kepshire (1979–80),

Joe Lahoud (1963–65), Mike Raczka (1981–84), Dave Schuler (1972–75), Stan Thomas (1969–71), Dave Wallace (1966–69)

Quinnipiac University (1)—Turk Wendell (1986–88)

Sacred Heart University (0)

Southern Connecticut State University (0)

Trinity College (3)—Jonah Bayliss (2000–02), Moe Drabowsky (1954–56), Ed Murray (1914–17)

Wesleyan University (1)—Lester A. (Red) Lanning (1913–16)

Western Connecticut State University (1)—Mike Porzio (1991–93)

Yale University (25)—Craig Breslow (2002–04), Johnny Broaca (1932), Ed Buckingham (1892–95), Bruce Caldwell (1927–28), Sam Childs (1883), Eddie Collins (1937–39), Ron Darling (1979–81), Bob Davis (1953–55), Pete Falsey (1910–14), Al Hubbard (1882–83), Bill Hutchison (1878–81), Jack Jones (1882–83), Ken MacKenzie (1955–56), Dick Manville (1945), Yale Murphy (1890–93), Denny O'Neil (1893), Queenie O'Rourke (1901), Spencer Pumpelly (1915–17), Frank Quinn (1945–48), Barney Reilly (1904–09), A.E. Smith (1882), Edgar Smith, Dick Tettelbach (1948–50), Bill Vinton (1884), Joe Wood (1939–41).

Two–Year Schools

Connecticut–Avery Point (1)—Rajai Davis

Norwalk Community College (1)—Erik Bedard

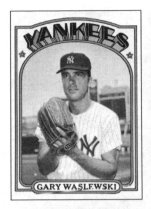

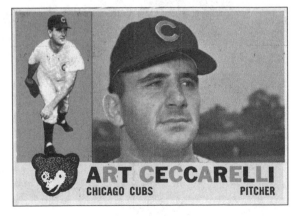

Top: Gary Waslewski, Berlin. *1972 Topps*; Carl Pavano, Southington. *1998 Topps*; Steve Bedrosian, University of New Haven. *1990 Donruss*.
Middle: Bob Saverine, Darien. *1968 Topps*; Keefe Cato, Fairfield University. *1985 Topps*.
Bottom: Walt "Monk" Dubiel, Hartford Public. *1951 Bowman*; Art Ceccarelli, West Haven. *1960 Topps*.

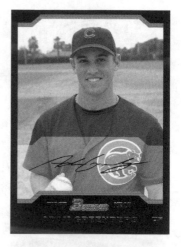

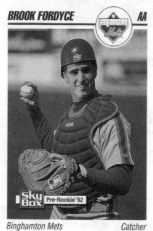

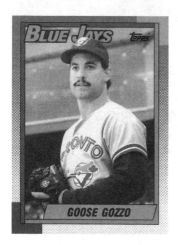

Clockwise from top left: Jason Grabowski, Clinton. *2001 Bowman/Topps*; Adam Greenberg, Guilford. *2004 Bowman/Topps*; Paul Householder, North Haven. *1983 Topps*; Mauro "Goose" Gozzo, Berlin. *1990 Topps*; Brook Fordyce, St. Bernard. *1992 Skybox.*

CONNECTICUT NATIVES IN THE
BASEBALL HALL OF FAME

	CATEGORY	INDUCTED	CREDENTIALS
Roger Connor, Waterbury	Player	1976	.317, 138 HR
Orator Jim O'Rourke, Bridgeport	Player	1945	.310, 2,304 hits
Edward "Ned" Hanlon, Montville	Manager	1996	Won 5 NL pennants
George Weiss, New Haven	Executive	1971	Built Yankee dynasty
Morgan G. Bulkeley, East Haddam	Executive	1937	First NL President

WORLD SERIES PARTICIPANTS

	TEAM	YEAR	G	HR/ BA
Brad Ausmus, Cheshire	Houston	2005	4	0 .250
Jack Barry, Meriden	Philadelphia AL, Boston AL	1910, '11, '13, '14, '15	25	0 .241
George "Kiddo" Davis, Bridgeport	New York NL	1933, '36	9	0 .381
Billy Gardner, Waterford	New York AL	1961	1	0 .000
Danny Hoffman, Canton	Philadelphia AL	1905	1	0 .000
Jay Johnstone, Manchester	New York AL, Los Angeles NL	1978, '81	5	1 .400
Larry Kopf, Bristol	Cincinnati	1919	8	0 .222
George "Candy" LaChance, Putnam	Boston AL	1903	8	0 .240
Dick McAuliffe, Farmington	Detroit	1968	7	1 .222
Matty McIntyre, Stonington	Detroit	1908, '09	9	0 .190

Johnny Moore, Waterville	Chicago NL	1932	2	0 .000
Tom Shopay, Bristol	Baltimore	1971	5	0 .000
Tim Teufel, Greenwich	New York NL	1986	3	1 .444

Pitchers

	TEAM	YEAR	G	W-L / ERA
Steve Blass, Canaan	Pittsburgh	1971	2	2–0 / 1.00
Rob Dibble, Southington	Cincinnati	1990	3	1–0 / 0.00
Joey Jay, Middletown	Cincinnati	1961	2	1–1 / 5.59
Charles Nagy, Fairfield	Cleveland	1995, '97	3	0–1 / 6.43
Carl Pavano, Southington	Florida	2003	2	0–0 / 1.00
Freddy Schmidt, Hartford	St. Louis NL	1944	1	0–0 / 0.00
Frank "Spec" Shea, Naugatuck	New York AL	1947	3	2–0 / 2.35
Rollie Sheldon, Putnam	New York AL	1964	2	0–0 / 0.00
Gary Waslewski, Meriden	Boston AL	1967	2	0–0 / 2.16

Managers

	TEAM	YEAR	RESULT
Bobby Valentine, Stamford	New York, NL	2000	Lost to Yankees, 4–1

ALL-STAR GAME PARTICIPANTS

	TEAM	YEAR	HIGHLIGHT
Brad Ausmus, Cheshire	Detroit	1999	0–1 at bat
Steve Blass, Canaan	Pittsburgh	1972	1 inning, 1 run
Ricky Bottalico, New Britain	Philadelphia	1996	1 scoreless inning
Bill Dawley, Lisbon	Houston	1983	1.1 scoreless innings
Rob Dibble, Southington	Cincinnati	1990, '91	2 scoreless innings
Walt Dropo, Moosup	Boston AL	1950	Triple in 3 at bats

Records

Dick McAuliffe, Farmington	Detroit	1965, '66, '67	2–9 at bat w/ home run
Charles Nagy, Fairfield	Cleveland	1992, '96	Losing pitcher, 1996
Carl Pavano, Southington	Florida	2004	2 innings, 2 runs
Jimmy Piersall, Waterbury	Boston AL	1954, '56	0–2 at bat
Frank "Spec" Shea, Naugatuck	New York AL	1947	First rookie winning pitcher
Mo Vaughn, Norwalk	Boston AL	1995, '96	1–5 at bat

AWARD WINNERS

	TEAM	YEAR	HIGHLIGHTS

Most Valuable Player

Mo Vaughn, 1B, Norwalk	Boston AL	1995	.300, 39 HR, 126 RBI

Sporting News All-Star Team

Joey Jay, P, Middletown	Cincinnati	1961	21–10 W-L, 3.53 ERA
Mo Vaughn, 1B, Norwalk	Boston AL	1995	.300, 39 HR, 126 RBI

Rookie of the Year

Walt Dropo, 1B, Moosup	Boston AL	1950	.322, 34 HR, 144 RBI

Co-MVP, National League Championship Series

Rob Dibble, P, Southington	Cincinnati	1990	5 IP, 10 SO, 0.00 ERA

	TEAM	YEAR	POSITION

Gold Glove

Jimmy Piersall, Waterbury	Boston AL	1958	Center field
Jimmy Piersall, Waterbury	Cleveland	1961	Center field
Brad Ausmus	Houston	2001	Catcher
Brad Ausmus	Houston	2002	Catcher
Brad Ausmus	Houston	2006	Catcher

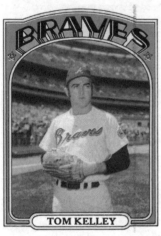

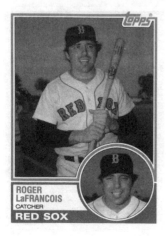

Records

LEAGUE LEADERS

Batting
Batting Average

	TEAM	YEAR	HIGHLIGHTS
Roger Connor, Waterbury	New York NL	1885	.371

Home Runs

	TEAM	YEAR	HIGHLIGHTS
Jim O'Rourke, Bridgeport	Boston NL	1880	6T
Roger Connor, Waterbury	New York PL	1890	14

Runs Batted In

	TEAM	YEAR	HIGHLIGHTS
Jim O'Rourke, Bridgeport	Boston NL	1879	62T
Roger Connor, Waterbury	New York NL	1889	130
Walt Dropo, Moosup	Boston AL	1950	144T
Mo Vaughn, Norwalk	Boston AL	1995	126T

Runs Scored

	TEAM	YEAR	HIGHLIGHTS
Jim O'Rourke, Bridgeport	Boston NL	1877	68
Matty McIntyre, Stonington	Detroit	1908	105
Dick McAuliffe, Farmington	Detroit	1968	95

Hits

	TEAM	YEAR	HIGHLIGHTS
Jim O'Rourke, Bridgeport	Buffalo NL	1884	162
Roger Connor, Waterbury	New York NL	1885	169

Triples

	TEAM	YEAR	HIGHLIGHTS
Roger Connor, Waterbury	Troy NL	1882	18
Jim O'Rourke, Bridgeport	New York NL	1885	16
Roger Connor, Waterbury	New York NL	1886	20

Doubles

	TEAM	YEAR	HIGHLIGHTS
Roger Connor, Waterbury	Philadelphia NL	1892	37
Jimmy Piersall, Waterbury	Boston AL	1956	40
Billy Gardner, Waterford	Baltimore	1957	36T

Opposite, clockwise from top left: Joey Jay, Woodrow Wilson. *1965 Topps*; Brian Looney, Cheshire. *1994 Fleer*; John McDonald, East Lyme. *2007 Topps*; Matt Merullo, Fairfield Prep. *1992 Donruss/Leaf*; Roger LaFrancois, Griswold. *1983 Topps*; Tom Kelley, Manchester. *1972 Topps*.

APPENDIX

Singles

| Matty McIntyre, Stonington | Detroit | 1908 | 131T |

Total Bases

| Roger Connor, Waterbury | New York NL | 1885 | 225 |
| Walt Dropo, Moosup | Boston AL | 1950 | 326 |

Slugging Percentage

Jim O'Rourke, Bridgeport	Boston NL	1879	.521
Roger Connor, Waterbury	New York NL	1889	.528
Roger Connor, Waterbury	New York PL	1890	.548

Stolen Bases

| Danny Hoffman, Canton | Philadelphia AL | 1905 | 46 |

Pitching

Victories

Bill Hutchison, New Haven	Chicago NL	1890	42
Bill Hutchison, New Haven	Chicago NL	1891	44
Bill Hutchison, New Haven	Chicago NL	1892	37
Joey Jay, Middletown	Cincinnati	1961	21T

Winning Percentage

Fred Goldsmith, New Haven	Chicago NL	1880	.875 (21–3)
Fred Klobedanz, Waterbury	Boston NL	1897	.788 (26–7)
Frank "Spec" Shea, Naugatuck	New York AL	1947	.737 (14–5)
Steve Blass, Canaan	Pittsburgh	1968	.750 (18–6)
Charles Nagy, Fairfield	Cleveland	1996	.773 (17–5)

Strikeouts

| Bill Hutchison, New Haven | Chicago NL | 1892 | 316 |

Shutouts

| Joey Jay, Middletown | Cincinnati | 1961 | 4T |
| Steve Blass, Canaan | Pittsburgh | 1971 | 5T |

Innings

Bill Hutchison, New Haven	Chicago NL	1890	603
Bill Hutchison, New Haven	Chicago NL	1891	561
Bill Hutchison, New Haven	Chicago NL	1892	627

Records

Games

Bill Hutchison, New Haven	Chicago NL	1890	71
Bill Hutchison, New Haven	Chicago NL	1891	66
Bill Hutchison, New Haven	Chicago NL	1892	75
Red Donahue, Waterbury	St. Louis NL	1897	42

Complete Games

Bill Hutchison, New Haven	Chicago NL	1890	65
Bill Hutchison, New Haven	Chicago NL	1891	56
Bill Hutchison, New Haven	Chicago NL	1892	67
Red Donahue, Waterbury	St. Louis NL	1897	38

OUTSTANDING PERFORMANCES

Batting

Three Home Runs in a Game

Roger Connor, Waterbury	New York NL v. Indianapolis, May 9, 1888
Johnny Moore, Waterville	Philadelphia NL v. Pittsburgh, July 22, 1936
Joe Lahoud, Danbury	Boston AL at Minnesota, June 11, 1969
Mo Vaughn, Norwalk	Boston AL v. Baltimore, September 24, 1996
Mo Vaughn, Norwalk	Boston AL v. New York, May 30, 1997

Six Hits in One Game

Roger Connor, Waterbury	St. Louis NL at New York, June 1, 1895
Jimmy Piersall, Waterbury	Boston AL at St. Louis, June 10, 1953

Most Consecutive Hits, Season

Walt Dropo, Moosup	Detroit, July 14, 15, 15, 1952 (12 hits, shares major league record)

Hitting for the Cycle (Single, Double, Triple, Home Run in game)

Jim O'Rourke, Bridgeport	Buffalo NL, June 16, 1884
Roger Connor, Waterbury	New York PL, July 21, 1890

Pitching

No-Hitters

Red Donahue, Waterbury	Philadelphia NL v. Boston, July 8, 1898 (W 5–0)

APPENDIX

Two Complete Games, Same Day

| Bill Hutchison, New Haven | Chicago NL, May 30, 1890 (W 6–4, W 11–7) |

Winning Streak by Pitcher

| Fred Klobedanz, Waterbury | Boston NL, 1897 (13 games) |

Fielding

Most Double Plays by First Baseman, Doubleheader (18 innings)

| Walt Dropo, Moosup | Boston AL, June 25, 1950 (8, shares major league record) |

Most Putouts by Second Baseman, Extra-Inning Game

| Billy Gardner, Waterford | Baltimore, May 21, 1957 (12 in 16 innings, shares American League record) |

Most Putouts by Shortstop, Nine-Inning Game

| Hod Ford, New Haven | Cincinnati, September 18, 1929 (11, shares major league record) |

Most Assists by Shortstop, Nine-Inning Game

| Tommy Corcoran, New Haven | Cincinnati, Aug. 7, 1903 (14, major league record) |

Most Double Plays Started by Shortstop, Game

| Larry Kopf, Bristol | Boston NL, April 28, 1922 (4, shares National League record) |

SINGLE-SEASON HIGHS

Since 1900

Batting

	TEAM	AVERAGE	YEAR
Batting Average—Mo Vaughn, Norwalk	Boston AL	.337	1998
Home Runs—Mo Vaughn, Norwalk	Boston AL	44	1996
Runs Batted In—Walt Dropo, Moosup	Boston AL	144	1950
Runs Scored—Mo Vaughn, Norwalk	Boston AL	118	1996
Hits—Mo Vaughn, Norwalk	Boston AL	207	1996

Records

Total Bases—Mo Vaughn, Norwalk	Boston AL	370	1996
Doubles—Jimmy Piersall, Waterbury	Boston AL	40	1956
Triples—Matty McIntyre, Stonington	Detroit	13	1908
Stolen Bases—Danny Hoffman, Canton	Philadelphia AL	46	1905

Pitching

Victories—Red Donahue, Waterbury	St. Louis AL	22	1902
Winning Percentage—Charles Nagy, Fairfield	Cleveland	.773	1996
Earned Run Average—Steve Blass, Canaan	Pittsburgh	2.12	1968
Strikeouts—Charles Nagy, Fairfield	Cleveland	169	1992
Complete Games—Red Donahue, Waterbury	Philadelphia NL	34	1901
Innings Pitched—Red Donahue, Waterbury	St. Louis AL	316	1902
Shutouts—Steve Blass, Canaan	Pittsburgh	7	1968
Saves—Ricky Bottalico, New Britain	Philadelphia	34	1996, 1997

BIBLIOGRAPHY

BOOKS

A.G. Spalding Company. *Spalding's Official Base Ball Guide, 1905*. Chicago: A.G. Spalding & Bros., 1905.

Appel, Martin, and Burt Goldblatt. *Baseball's Best: The Hall of Fame Gallery*. New York: McGraw-Hill Book Company, 1977.

Bielawa, Michael J. *Bridgeport Baseball*. Charleston, SC: Arcadia Publishing, 2003.

Bodendieck, Zack, and Tom Gatto. *2007 Baseball Register*. Chesterfield, MO: The Sporting News, 2007.

Jones, David. *Deadball Stars of the American League*. Dulles, VA: Potomac Books, Inc., 2006.

Jordan, Pat. *The Suitors of Spring*. New York: Dodd, Mead & Company, 1970.

Kiersh, Edward. *Where Have You Gone, Vince DiMaggio?* New York: Bantam Books, 1983.

MacFarlane, Paul, in collaboration with Leonard Gettelson. *Daguerreotypes of Great Stars of Baseball*. St. Louis: The Sporting News, 1968.

Major League Baseball. *The Baseball Encyclopedia*. 10th Edition. New York: Macmillan, 1996.

Marazzi, Rich, and Len Fiorito. *Aaron to Zipfel*. New York: Avon Books, 1985.

Roer, Mike. *Baseball in Bridgeport: From Barnum to Bluefish*. N.p.: The Academy Group, 1998.

Rubin, Sam. *Baseball in New Haven*. Charleston, SC: Arcadia Publishing, 2003.

Weiss, Bill, and Marshall Wright. *The 100 Greatest Minor League Baseball Teams of the 20th Century*. Parker, CO: Outskirts Press, 2006.

PERIODICALS

Harrison, Don. "Guglielmo hollers 'foul!'" *Waterbury Republican*, April 22, 1979.

———. "Minor League Ball Finally Finds a Niche." *New York Times*, October 16, 1994.

King, Chris. "The Forgotten Home Team in Hartford." *New York Times*, April 13, 2003.

Palladino, Joe. "Waterbury Team Ruled…in 1884." *Waterbury Republican-American*, March 30, 2008.

Solomon, Deborah. "Questions for Bobby Valentine." *New York Times Sunday Magazine*, May 4, 2008.

Watson, Elbert L. "Bert Shepard was a hero in the air and on the bases." *Times Examiner*, May 7, 2008.

ABOUT THE AUTHOR

Twin passions—newspapers and baseball— provided the impetus for Don Harrison's early career in sportswriting. In a sense, they have led to *Connecticut Baseball*, his new book about the Nutmeg State's myriad contributions to Major League Baseball.

An award-winning sports editor with the *Waterbury Republican-American*, Harrison chronicled nine World Series, covered the game's spring training camps in Florida and conducted interviews with many of the sport's luminaries. Long before he became a member of the Society for American Baseball Research (SABR), he put his expertise to work as a contributor to two editions of *The Official Encyclopedia of Baseball*.

Don's freelance articles have appeared in the *Sporting News*, *Sports Quarterly-Baseball*, the *New York Times*, *Connecticut* magazine and dozens of other publications. He is the author of *25 Years Plus One*, which captured Fairfield University's meteoric rise in men's basketball, and a contributing author to two editions of *Inside Women's College Basketball*.

Harrison's career in public relations embraces work with a corporation in Fairfield County and Sacred Heart University, where he was the founding editor of the college's quarterly magazine. He earned an undergraduate degree from Sacred Heart.

In 2002, he became a founding editor for the second time when he spearheaded the launch of the *Greenwich Citizen*, a weekly newspaper in Fairfield County. The *Citizen* has won several awards from the New England Press Association (NEPA), including one for General Excellence.

Don and his wife, Patti, live in Fairfield, Connecticut. They are the parents of three grown children, Rachel Anderson, Erin Harrison French and Alexis P. Harrison, and the grandparents of Lauren Elizabeth French and Luke Charles Anderson.